Policy Deployment

Also available from Quality Press

Management by Policy: How Companies Focus Their Total Quality Efforts to Achieve Competitive Advantage
Brendan Collins and Ernest Huge

Integrated Process Management: A Quality Model
Roger Slater

Ethics in Quality
August B. Mundel

Quality Management Benchmark Assessment
J. P. Russell

A Guide to Graphical Problem-Solving Process
John W. Moran, Richard P. Talbot, and Russell M. Benson

Benchmarking: The Search for Industry Best Practices that Lead to Superior Performance
Robert C. Camp

QFD: A Practitioner's Approach
James L. Bossert

To request a complimentary catalog of publications, call 800-248-1946.

Policy Deployment

The TQM Approach to Long-Range Planning

Bruce M. Sheridan

ASQC Quality Press
Milwaukee, Wisconsin

Policy Deployment: The TQM Approach to Long-Range Planning
Bruce M. Sheridan

Library of Congress Cataloging-in-Publication-Data

Sheridan, Bruce M.
   Policy deployment: the TQM approach to long-range planning/
Bruce M. Sheridan.
     p. cm.
   Includes bibliographical references and index.
   ISBN 0-87389-129-5 (alk. paper)
   1. Total quality management. 2. Total quality management—Case
studies. 3. FPL (Florida: Firm)—Management. I. Title.
HD62.15.S545 1993
658.5'62—dc20   93-4040
                                          CIP

10 9 8 7 6 5 4 3 2 1

ISBN 0-87389-129-5

Acquisitions Editor: Susan Westergard
Production Editor: Annette Wall
Marketing Administrator: Mark Olson
Set in Garamond and Helvetica Condensed by Montgomery Media, Inc.
Cover design by Montgomery Media, Inc.
Printed by BookCrafters, Inc.

ASQC Mission: To facilitate continuous improvement and increase customer satisfaction by identifying, communicating, and promoting the use of quality principles, concepts, and technologies; and thereby be recognized throughout the world as the leading authority on, and champion for, quality.

For a free copy of the ASQC Quality Press Publications Catalog, including ASQC membership information, call 800-248-1946.

Printed in the United States of America

 Printed on acid-free recycled paper

 ASQC
Quality Press
611 East Wisconsin Avenue
Milwaukee, Wisconsin 53202

Dedicated to Jan Emily

Contents

Acknowledgments

I would not have been able to complete this work without the assistance of the Florida Power and Light Company and the Union of Japanese Scientists and Engineers. To both organizations, I thank you.

The following professors from the University of Miami and the University of Miami Quality Institute provided valuable input: Dr. Tarek Khalil, Dr. Shihab Asfour, Dr. Harold Berkman, Dr. Howard Gitlow, and Dr. David Sumanth.

Mr. Randy Castleberry, chief executive officer of SPATCO, had the foresight to recognize the positive impact of embracing TQM as a management philosophy. I have thoroughly enjoyed working with Randy and SPATCO's other executives and employees in implementing TQM.

Special thanks to Brendan Collins, Noriaki Kano, and Irwin Weinberg.

Introduction

A review of several management theories is presented in this book, concluding with the theory of total quality management. Subsequently, a detailed outline of the total quality management process is developed. This outline is used to review how the management services department of Florida Power and Light Company, winner of the prestigious Deming Prize, has implemented its total quality management process.

Policy deployment is the first process of total quality management. A procedure for an organization to implement policy deployment is developed. This is followed by two case studies. The first presents Florida Power and Light's policy deployment process. It is the process any large corporation could implement. The second case study presents the process a small business can use. SPATCO is a small business that distributes liquid handling equipment and provides environmental services.

A how-to procedure for implementing policy deployment is presented in this text. For an organization implementing total quality management, it is a must.

1

Text Road Map

In the late 1970s and throughout the 1980s, it had become evident to many American industries that the products imported from foreign countries were of better quality than their American counterparts. Consequently, the current approach to addressing this issue is to implement a quality program and hope it works. The words *quality* and *productivity* appear in many American advertisements. Presently, a concern exists whether these quality and productivity programs are producing the desired result.

In 1989, for the first time in U.S. history, a Japanese automobile was the best-selling car.

The Top Ten[1]

1989	1978
Honda Accord	Chevrolet (full-size)
Ford Taurus	Oldsmobile Cutlass Supreme
Ford Escort	Ford Fairmont
Chevrolet Corsica/Beretta	Chevrolet Malibu
Chevrolet Cavalier	Chevrolet Monte Carlo
Toyota Camry	Fort LTD
Ford Tempo	Ford Thunderbird
Nissan Sentra	Olds 88
Pontiac Grand Am	Chevrolet Camaro
Toyota Corolla	Cadillac

In the late 1950s and 1960s, American industries were world leaders. Many management systems have been tried since then, including vocational training, the "big happy family" approach, behavioral science, management by objectives, and so on. They seem to have come and gone, leaving American industry in its present state. Were any of these techniques successful? If so, how did a particular corporation measure its implementation and success of a management system? American management does fine implementing a new management technique, but performs poorly when checking or measuring how successfully a management technique has been implemented.

With the increasing number of firms implementing a total quality management (TQM) process, a need exists to know how well these processes are producing the desired result. The following definition of TQM is from the Union of Japanese Scientists and Engineers (JUSE):

> A system of means whereby the qualities of products or services are produced economically to meet the requirements of the purchaser. "Quality Control" is sometimes called "QC" for short. In addition, since modern quality control adopts statistical techniques, it is sometimes especially called "Statistical Quality Control", and "SQC" for short. In order to perform quality control effectively, throughout all phases of the enterprise activities such as market survey, research and development, planning of product, design, production readiness, procurement and subcontract, manufacture, inspection, sales and after sales servicing as well as finance, personnel affairs and indoctrination, whole [organization's entire] personnel including from the executives down to the managers, foremen and workers are required to participate and collaborate. The quality control activities conducted in such [a] way is called "Company-Wide Quality Control" and "CWQC" for short or "Total Quality Control", and "TQC" for short.[2]

In this definition, JUSE uses the term Total Quality Control (TQC). In my opinion, TQM and TQC have the same meaning. I simply prefer the word *management* over the word *control*. Throughout this text TQM will be used to refer to a quality control process involving all aspects of an organization's operation.

America has the opportunity to improve management's understanding of TQM process implementation. If a corporation implements the TQM process properly, the process itself provides the means to measure how well it is performing. The TQM process uses data to measure its own progress continuously.

JUSE uses 10 criteria to evaluate an organization's TQM process. Policy deployment is one of the ten criteria. Implementing policy stimulates an organization to identify and *quantify* its needs. Most companies do not have systems in place nor the understanding to implement policy deployment fully. Thus, American industry has a tremendous opportunity to improve its TQM process by properly implementing policy deployment.

The objective of this text is to develop a procedure to implement policy deployment for a TQM process. This objective will be achieved through the following steps:

1. A review of the literature of current management systems. This will include research of the current systems used to measure the effectiveness of TQM processes.
2. Development of a procedure to implement policy deployment for a TQM process. A case study of a major U.S. corporation's implementation of policy deployment will be presented. This will be followed by a case study of a small business' implementation of policy deployment.
3. Development of a TQM process checklist of the 10 Deming Prize criteria required by JUSE.
4. A comparative case study of a major U.S. corporation's TQM process compared to the TQM process checklist developed. This will provide an example of how an overall TQM process is implemented.

The first step toward attaining the objectives is to determine which TQM process to use. Through the research of current literature, the Deming Prize criteria was selected as an effective TQM process. The Deming Prize is awarded annually by JUSE.

The objective of writing a procedure to implement policy deployment is undertaken. This is followed by a review of the fundamentals of TQM. The policy deployment procedure is written in a generic format and can be adapted to any type of organization.

A study of the Kansai Electric Company in Japan and the Florida Power and Light (FPL) Company is conducted. Research of the methodology Kansai Electric Company used to become the first utility to receive the Deming Application Prize in 1984 will serve to produce a checklist to review a department within FPL. FPL, the first U.S. company (utility or otherwise) to win the Deming Application Prize for Overseas Companies in November 1989, has been using the TQM process since 1981. (An interesting point is that Kansai Electric does not have union employees, whereas FPL does.)

During a two-hour meeting with Dr. Tarek Khalil, University of Miami, and Dr. Noriaki Kano, JUSE counselor and member of the Deming Prize Committee, FPL's management services department was selected as the area to study. It was believed that a corporatewide analysis would be too broad and too difficult. The study of a single department would provide more detail and meaningful research versus a general overview of the entire organization.

I worked in the management services department from February 1987 to January 1991 and was directly involved in the application of the TQM process at FPL for over eight years.

In 1985, I designed and implemented a pilot policy deployment program at FPL. At the time, it was referred to as enhanced management by objectives. Trying to understand exactly how to implement policy deployment was difficult and frustrating. Imagine someone asking you to bring him or her a rock, providing you with no additional information. So you gather up what you think is a nice rock. Upon presenting it, the individual informs you it is not the right rock. What you come to find out is that you will never bring the right rock although you can continuously improve upon the previous one. This is similar to the policy deployment process. Continuous improvement is an integral part of the process. Accepting the fact that it will never be perfect early in the implementation phase of policy deployment will eliminate some of the frustration.

In addition to FPL's policy deployment case study, a second case study is presented involving SPATCO, a small distributor based in the southeastern United States. SPATCO was founded in 1932 as a family business. Over the life of the organization, many management styles have come and gone. In January 1990, SPATCO measured its customer satisfaction in the liquid process technology division, one of three divisions. This began SPATCO's use of TQM.

2
History of Management

In the *Handbook for Professional Managers*, management is defined as "an integrating process by which authorized individuals create, maintain, and operate an organization in the selection and accomplishment of its aims."[3] Exactly when the practice of management began is unclear. "The practice of management is as old as organizations, which makes it very old indeed. Clay tablets dating back to 3000 B.C. record business transactions and laws in ancient Sumeria. . . ."[4] Documentation on or the study of these earlier management systems is minimal. One particular organization that began in 200 to 300 A.D. was the Roman Catholic Church. It is a notable example of a management system that is still prosperous today. "The simple structure—pope, cardinal, archbishop, bishop, parish priest—chosen by the church's founders and still used today is more modern than structures of many organizations begun this year."[5]

"The activity of management is ancient, but formal study of the discipline of management is relatively new."[6] Management historians place the start of the formal study of management in the 1800s. For example, Robert Owen studied management in 1800s and Andrew Ure in 1835.

> Early civilizations reflected some early attempts to relate individuals to organizations but generally placed a low value on economic activity and held a parochial view of the management function. The cultural rebirth brought a new view of people, of economic activity, of social values, of political arrangements, and established the preconditions for the Industrial Revolution.[7]

Many credit Frederick W. Taylor with starting the process of scientific management. He is often referred to as the father of scientific management. Taylor was employed at Midvale Steel in Philadelphia, Pennsylvania, from 1878 to 1890. He started scientific management ". . . by using observation, measurement, logic, and analysis . . . [to] . . . redesign many manual tasks to make them far more efficient."[8] In 1911, Frederick W. Taylor published *Principles of Scientific Management: 1911*. "Management's emergence as a discipline, a field of scholarly inquiry and research, was partly a response to big business' needs, partly an effort to reap more of the benefits of technology created during the Industrial Revolution, and partly the achievement of a handful of curious individuals with a burning interest in finding the most efficient way of accomplishing a job."[9] "For the first time in history, problems of managing large-scale organizations became widespread as individual and commercial enterprises began to replace individual proprietors and partnerships as the usual forms of business."[10]

In the early 1900s, the classical or administrative management theory began to emerge. Henri Fayol developed the 14 Principles of Management, which he felt could be used to plan, organize, command, coordinate, and control—in other words, to administer an organization. "The classical school's objective was to identify universal principles of management applicable to all organizations."[11]

From 1920 to 1940, human relations theory was the prevailing management style. The management scientists of the time, such as Elton Mayo, believed that ". . . if management showed more concern for their employees, employee satisfaction should increase, which would lead to an increase in productivity. They recommend the use of human relations techniques such as more effective supervision, employee counseling, and giving workers more opportunities to communicate on the job."[12]

In this same time frame, the Hawthorne experiments made a significant discovery. The Hawthorne experiments studied the productivity of workers in a plant environment and found that "output was not related to physical conditions of work but to how people were treated and how they felt about their work, their supervisors, and their coworkers."[13] This was such a profound finding that Harvard University set up a research center to further study this theory. Thus, it was the birth of behavioral science as a management system.

All this research, combined with the rebirth of the administrative management theory, led to the development of numerous management systems. "There are, as we shall learn, no universally applicable techniques or firm principles for managing effectively." [14] Since 1950, the numerous management systems available are referred to under the heading management science. "The modern era demanded that managers refine their decision-making methods, that they enlarge their conceptual schema, and that they seek better ways of allocating and utilizing their physical and human resources. . . . In management science, the search was for order, for management, and for predictability." [15] A discussion of management science theories follows.

BEHAVIORAL SCIENCE (1950s)

In 1949, Chester Bernard wrote a paper on behavioral science. In the 1950s, extensive work in this area was also conducted by Abraham Maslow, Douglas McGregor, and Frederick Herzberg. "In basic terms, the aim of the behavioral science school was to increase organizational effectiveness by increasing the effectiveness of its human resources." [16]

OPERATIONS RESEARCH (1950s)

Operations research originated from military practices.

> Operations research is the systematic application of quantitative methods, techniques, and tools to the analysis of problems involving the operation of systems. . . . most operations research projects involve the optimization of some operations of a system, such as minimizing production costs, maximizing profits, maximizing the capacity of a flow (of goods or information) through some network, or minimizing the cost of achieving certain technical properties for some engineering entity or operation. [17]

Combined with operations research is the theory of the quantitative approach. This theory resulted in the "development of quantitative techniques to help managers make decisions in complex situations." [18] These quantitative techniques were used to develop models. Management then applied the models to complex problems to assist them in making decisions to solve these problems.

PROCESS APPROACH (1950s)

This theory is a result of revisiting Fayol's administrative theory. It considers the management functions to be interdependent. "The management process as a whole consists of four interrelated functions: planning, organizing, motivating, and controlling." [19]

MANAGEMENT BY OBJECTIVES (1954)

> Management by objectives [MBO] requires major effort and special instruments. For in the business enterprise managers are not automatically directed toward a common goal. On the contrary, business, by its very nature, contains three powerful factors of misdirection: in the specialized work of most managers; in the hierarchical structure of management; and in the differences in vision and work and the resultant insulation of various levels of management. [20]

> "MBO is a participative system of managing in which managers look ahead for improvements, think strategically, set performance stretch objectives at the beginning of a time period, develop action and supporting plans, and ensure accountability for results at the end of the time period." [21]

> MBO theory is complex. It is eclectic, that is, it is a selection and synthesis of managerial elements from five schools of thought: economic theory, process theory, systems theory, quantitative theory, and behavioral theory. The selection and synthesis are based on the situation at hand or the situation to be created. [22]

SYSTEMS APPROACH (1960s)

"The application of systems theory to management has made it easier for managers to conceptualize the organization as an entity of interrelated parts that is inexorably intertwined with the outside world." [23] "Using the systems approach, the managers define system objectives, establish criteria for evaluating systems performance, and better relate the firm to a variety of environmental systems." [24]

LEADERSHIP THEORY (MID 1960s)

Use of this theory lets managers identify their current style of leadership. Steps are then outlined to assist managers to adjust their style to become more effective leaders. Fred Fiedler was a strong advocate of the leadership model. He was the author of *A Theory of Leadership Effectiveness,* published in 1967.

CONTINGENCY APPROACH (MANAGEMENT THEORY JUNGLE) (1968)

"That the theory and science of management are far from being mature is apparent in the continuation of the management theory jungle." [25]
"The focal point of the contingency approach is the situation, the specific set of circumstances that influence the organization most at a particular time." [26] "The contingency approach tries to match specific techniques or concepts of managing to the specific situation at hand in order to attain organizational objectives most effectively." [27]

PARTICIPATORY MANAGEMENT/ORGANIZATIONAL BEHAVIOR (1970s)

"Advocates of industrial democracy have generally not been primarily concerned about the desires of workers for increased participation. Consequently, very little is known about the relationship between individual characteristics of workers and their belief in participation." [28] "Operating on the premise that worker participation would yield a greater commitment to organizational goals and would also further individual and group satisfaction, researchers sought to design work arrangements which would permit the involvement of subordinates in decision making." [29]

> Our continuing research on the purpose and process of participative management has, in our view, contributed additional support for the Human Resources theory of participation. It has emphasized that when the impact on

subordinates is considered, the superior's attitude toward the traits and abilities of his subordinates is equally as important as the amount of consultation in which he engages.[30]

Along the lines of participative management theory is the organizational behavior theory. "It seems clear that if democratic voting is to be instrumentally effective then it has to be extended into organizations which vitally affect the interests of every citizen, yet which, being seen as private, are responsible only to themselves."[31] "Depending on their specific conditions, some capitalistic firms may be able to introduce limited degrees of worker participation, but it is unlikely that the full motivational and organizational benefits of worker control will ever be experienced under capitalism."[32] "As our understanding of human behavior increases or as new social conditions develop, our organizational behavior models are also likely to change. It is a grave mistake to assume that one particular model is a best model which will endure for the long run."[33]

MANAGEMENT BY EXCEPTION (1970s)

Management by Exception is a method of using exceptions to control the operation. It can be the culmination of an operating system, where interruptions to the completion of a plan are identified at the point of initial execution. These interruptions or exceptions can be collected and carried forward to all levels of management. If properly identified and grouped, these exceptions can be either eliminated or must be included in future plans. Management by Exception is the method of making management face the impact of problems.[34]

Having an original plan in place is very important. "Establish the plan—this is the first and most important rule in any system of Management Control by Exception."[35] The next step is to develop a chain of command. Once the chain of command is developed, the plan is reviewed carefully. A system of exception reporting is set up and the plan is revised based on these exceptions. "What we are seeking in the use of Management by Exception Systems is, quite basically, that information we do not know. Such information tells us what must be done to improve. This simple truth is so often overlooked in so many companies."[36]

STRATEGIC MANAGEMENT (1970 TO 1990s)

Strategic Management is the decision-making process that formulates strategic plans, acquires resources, allocates resources to organizational units, and uses strategic control to ensure that the goals and objectives are achieved. Strategic Management deals with an organization's capability to cope with a dynamic and often turbulent environment. It uses a total-system perspective to integrate the key strategic factors of environmental demands, internal performance, resource requirements, and organizational considerations.[37]

Strategic management begins with a problem statement. An analysis of the problem is conducted and alternative solutions are formulated. These alternatives are evaluated and a strategy is developed. This strategy, or solution, is then implemented and controlled.

... the value of a strategy is that it can be articulated and communicated in understandable terms, that it can be analyzed, tested, and evaluated, for rejection, modification, or acceptance—before the competition takes place, before resources are committed and risks incurred, and before adverse results are realized.[38]

PRODUCTIVITY MANAGEMENT (1970 TO 1990s)

Productivity management is a formal management process involving all levels of management and employees with the ultimate objective of reducing the cost of the manufacturing, distributing, and selling of a product or service through an integration of the four phases of the productivity cycle, namely productivity measurement, evaluation, planning, and improvement.[39]

In addition to presenting the four phases of the productivity cycle, David J. Sumanth develops a detailed model used for productivity measurement. Referred to as the total productivity model (TPM), it provides a means to measure the total tangible output versus the total tangible input.

"Productivity planning is not a one-time action. It is a continuous process that requires total organizational involvement in constantly analyzing business trend patterns and formulating and implementing new objectives that provide competitive operating advantages for the organization."[40] Johnson Edosomwan depicts the productivity management process as a triangle. "The triangle . . . encompasses a system that provides for input of information relevant to the planning process, the performance and productivity measurement process, and implementation of corrective actions and techniques to improve productivity."[41]

THEORY Z (1980s TO 1990s)

In 1981, William Ouchi wrote the book *Theory Z, How American Business Can Meet the Japanese Challenge.*

> Theory Z organizations capture the best in management methods from Japanese and U.S. approaches. A Theory Z organization is egalitarian, engages fully the participation of employees in running the company, and emphasizes subtle concern in interpersonal relations. It is characterized by employee cooperation and commitment to the objectives of the company.[42]

This review of literature illustrates the many management systems available. A summary of all the management systems covered is presented in Table 2.1. Many arguments exist for and against each management system. The purpose of this research is not to delve into the differences between these numerous systems. Instead, a detailed review of yet another management system will be undertaken. Following the review, a procedure to implement a segment of this management system will be developed. The management system being referred to is TQM.

Table 2.1: Management systems review.

Management System	Approximate Time of Development
First studies	1800 to 1835
Scientific	Late 1800s
Administrative	Early 1900s
Human relations	1920 to 1940
Behavioral science	1930 to 1950
Operations research	1950s
Process approach	1950s
Management by objectives	1954
Systems approach	1960s
Leadership theory	Mid 1960s
Total quality control	Mid 1960s
Contingency approach	Late 1960s
Participative management	1970s
Management by exception	1970s
Strategic management	1970 to 1990s
Productivity management	1970 to 1990s
Theory Z	1980 to 1990s

3

Total Quality Management

OVERVIEW

"Credit for originating the term goes to an American, Armand V. Feigenbaum, in the 1961 book, *Total Quality Control*. Many Japanese prefer to speak of companywide quality control, or CWQC. But the meaning is the same."[43]

At this point, it would be advantageous to review JUSE's definition of TQM presented in chapter 1 (See page 2).

Quite frankly, it is difficult not to refer to Japan when discussing TQM. According to Kaoru Ishikawa, the following characteristics are what make Japanese TQM unique.

1. Companywide quality control; participation by all members of the organization in quality control
2. Education and training in quality control
3. Quality control circle activities
4. Quality control audits (Deming Application Prize and presidential audit)
5. Utilization of statistical methods
6. Nationwide quality control promotion activities[44]

The quality movement in Japan was started by JUSE in 1949. In 1950, W. Edwards Deming was invited by JUSE to Japan to lecture on quality. "Deming based his theories on the simple scientific observation that all processes suffer some level of variation, which is likely to diminish quality."[45] Another unique feature of the Deming philosophy is the emphasis he places on management.

Deming points out—as Dr. [Joseph M.] Juran has argued since the early 1950's—that at least 85 percent of the failures in any organi[z]ation are the fault of systems controlled by management. Fewer than 15 per cent of the problems are actually worker-related. Management, and management alone, is now responsible for the transformation of western business, he insists.[46]

Deming's management philosophy is based on the following 14 points:[47]

1. Create constancy of purpose toward improvement of product and service, with a plan to improve competitive position and stay in business.
2. Adopt the new philosophy. We are in a new economic age. We can no longer live with commonly accepted levels of delays, mistakes, defective materials, and defective workmanship.

> Customer satisfaction must become the focus of corporate thinking. Providing customers with goods and services that meet their expectations and needs at a price they are willing to pay is paramount.[48]

3. Cease dependence on mass inspection. Require, instead, statistical evidence that quality is built in to eliminate the need for inspection on a mass basis.
4. End the practice of awarding business on the basis of price tag. Instead, depend on meaningful measures of quality, along with price.
5. Find problems. It is management's job to work continually on improving the system.
6. Institute modern methods of training on the job.

> In the Deming philosophy, people are viewed as an organization's most valuable long-term resources. …Modern methods of training help to create the new corporate environment and provide a positive attitude that is necessary to compete and succeed in the new economic age.[49]

7. Institute modern methods of supervision.
8. Drive out fear so that everyone may work effectively for the company.

> Imagine waking up every morning, getting ready to go someplace that makes you feel insecure, anxious, afraid, and inadequate. You do this day after day, week after week, month after month, and finally, year after year. This kind of thing starts to take its toll. Your stress levels increase, your health deteriorates, your family relationships suffer, your job performance diminishes, and you burn out. [50]

9. Break down barriers between departments.

> Breaking down barriers requires a long-term perspective. These barriers were created over a long period of time, and it will take time and patience to remove them. [51]

10. Eliminate numerical goals, posters, and slogans that seek new levels of productivity without providing methods.

> Replacing arbitrary goals with the use of statistical methods, particularly control charts, will aid in strengthening management's credibility. Workers will begin to believe that they are not being pushed to produce, penalized for variation, or expected to bear the burden of management for taking responsibility for the system. [52]

11. Eliminate work standards that prescribe numerical quotas.
12. Remove barriers that rob employees of their pride of workmanship.
13. Institute a vigorous program of education and retraining.
14. Create a structure that will build on the prior 13 points every day.

If these 14 points are followed, Deming insists the organization will produce higher quality goods and services, increase productivity, decrease costs, improve the quality of work life, and, most importantly, stay in business.

The following excerpts are taken from recent articles on American and Canadian quality. "In the U.S., it took the rude shock of losing sales to foreign competitors in the early 1980s to convince manufacturers to embrace Deming and to adapt Japanese-like attention to quality."[53]

The following comments are from an article by K. Theodore Krantz, president of Velcro, U.S.A., regarding a meeting called by General Motors to discuss Velcro's quality (and continuation of its purchase order). "But they said our process was unacceptable: we were inspecting quality into the product, we were not manufacturing quality into the product."[54]

"All the auto companies have upgraded their [TQM processes] programs . . . and what was acceptable three years ago is no longer good enough."[55] "In the search for quality, there's no such thing as good enough; there's never a finish line."[56]

Norman B. Wright, president of Kepner-Tegroe, management consultants, discusses quality issues in Canada. In his article, Wright states the *best* reliability of a Hewlett-Packard 16K RAM component manufactured in North America was 1.8 percent unreliable while Japan was producing the same chip with a 0.3 percent unreliable rating. "The dominance of Japanese products in our markets is a force with which Canadian business must reckon."[57]

The final excerpt is from David A. Garvin's exploratory study regarding the differences in quality of air conditioners between U.S. and Japanese firms. He discovered the following:[58]

Air Conditioner Plant	Assembly Line Defects per 100 Units
Japanese plant	0.95
Best U.S. plants	9.00
Better U.S. plants	26.00
Fair U.S. plants	63.50
Poor U.S. plants	135.00

Anecdotal evidence suggests that at many U.S. companies, a different ethic developed (*Business Week*, 1982; Leonard & Sasser, 1982: 164–166). In the United States today, quality is often considered secondary to other goals. Few managers or workers are trained in the principles of quality control, and the connection between quality, productivity, and cost is often poorly understood. In these circumstances, the commitment of managers and workers to improving quality is likely to be much weaker than it is at comparable Japanese Companies.[59]

. . . that U.S. and Japanese manufacturers not only face different profiles of quality problems, but may also be approaching the task of quality management quite differently. According to supervisors, the Japanese firms in this sample displayed a strong management commitment to quality, organized their thinking around process control and production management, and had workers who demonstrated a clear concern for quality improvement, even without explicit goals to reduce prevailing levels of rework and scrap. Although these companies still faced quality problems, supervisors believed that most of them arose outside the shop floor, primarily in the areas of product design and purchased parts and materials.

By contrast, U.S. supervisors attributed the largest proportion of their firms' quality problems to deficiencies in workforce or workmanship. A deep concern for quality was thought to be lacking among workers and also among managers, even though supervisors were frequently evaluated on such measures as defect and scrap rates. Overall, U.S. supervisors believed that quality was a secondary or tertiary objective for manufacturing, lagging well behind the primary goal of meeting production schedules.[60]

This review of literature was presented to help readers understand the concept of TQM. Subsequent sections provide a more detailed study of the TQM process. This is initiated by reviewing the current systems used to measure the TQM process.

MEASURING A TQM PROCESS

In order to determine how to measure a TQM process, a review of two of the world's most prominent measurement systems will be undertaken.

JUSE sponsors the Deming Prize and the U.S. Department of Commerce sponsors the Malcolm Baldrige National Quality Award. Both of these will be reviewed keeping in mind their functions as assessment tools.

Deming Prize

A formal measurement of the entire TQM activity is performed by JUSE. A JUSE subcommittee—the Deming Prize Committee—conducts a complete examination of an organization's implementation of TQM.

In July 1950, W. Edwards Deming was invited to Japan to teach a quality control seminar. This was the beginning of a strong marriage between Japan and Deming's philosophy of statistical quality control. Due to Deming's education and the efforts of JUSE, Japan has become one of the most prominent and consistent producers of quality products and services. A significant contribution was also made by another American in 1954, namely Joseph M. Juran.

It became apparent to the JUSE organization that Dr. Deming was the catalyst Japan needed to rekindle the national quest to revive Japanese industry. Recognizing this, the late Kuichi Koyanagi, a board member and one of the founders of JUSE, proposed a formal resolution in 1951 to institute the Deming Prize. In recognition of Deming's friendship and achievement in the cause of industrial quality control, the JUSE board of directors approved the resolution.

The Deming Prize Committee issues an award for three categories.

1. The Deming Prize for Individual Person. This prize is granted to an individual who shows significant achievement in the theory or application of statistical quality control.
2. The Deming Application Prize is awarded to an enterprise that achieves the most distinctive improvement of performance through the application of statistical quality control. This award is further broken down into the Deming Application Prize for Small Enterprises and the Deming Application Prize for Division.
3. The Deming Application Prize for Overseas Companies. This is awarded to an overseas company that displays the meritorious implementation of TQM.

The head of the Deming Prize Committee is the chairman of the board of JUSE or a person approved by the board of directors. Members of the board of directors are usually professors and officers of organizations who possess exceptional TQM experience. An application prize subcommittee is formed to perform the evaluation of the various applicants' TQM processes. This subcommittee consists of professors and quality experts not employed by corporations. In order not to bring bias to the judging, these quality experts are solicited from government positions or nonprofit organizations.

Applicants must submit a detailed explanation of their TQM process. Based on this report, the application prize subcommittee determines if the organization warrants further review. If so, the next step is a series of on-site examinations. This audit is performed by the members of the application prize subcommittee. These examinations are performed impartially. The areas measured are as follows:

1. Policy
2. Organizational design
3. Education/training
4. Information
5. Analysis
6. Standardization
7. Control
8. Quality assurance
9. Effectiveness
10. Future plans

After the application prize subcommittee completes its site visits, the committee members will meet with the Deming Prize committee to discuss their findings. At this meeting, these quality experts discuss how each organization developed its TQM process. The committee members' objective is to determine if the organization applied the TQM principles to gain the maximum benefit for their organization. For example, Table 3.1 outlines a few of the areas two different industries would need to address. Thus, their TQM processes would be tailored to address these issues.

In comparing these two industries, the chemical plant needs to adhere to the specifications of a chemical process while the automobile manufacturer might put customer satisfaction and perceived value as its foremost concern. In other words, each industry will first need to identify which direction it wants its organization to pursue as part of applying TQM techniques. It is for this reason the Deming Prize committee chooses not to use a score sheet to review the organization in

Table 3.1: Different approaches to TQM.

Chemical plant	Automobile manufacturer
Rigid adherence to specifications (i.e., chemical formulas) Chemical quality control Batch processing	Extensive marketing Analysis of customer meeds Assembly line Parts quality control Competition

the final stage of review. Instead, a discussion of how well its TQM process supported the organization is the basis for determining if the Deming Prize is to be awarded. However, the application prize sub-committee uses a grading process during the preliminary judging. This grading process is performed in the strictest confidence, and the methodology of measurement is not released. The Deming Prize committee encourages the organizations to focus their attention on the TQM system and the use of statistical quality management rather than the acquisition of points.

In addition to determining how well a TQM process fits an organization, the Deming Prize committee will perform a detailed analysis of the use of statistical quality control. The use of statistical quality control encourages management to make decisions based on data. If an organization understands the concepts involved in the correct use of statistics, they can make decisions for improvement based on facts as opposed to opinions. Making decisions throughout the organization based on the use of statistical quality control, from entry-level employees to top management, is the cornerstone of a sound TQM process.

Finally, the Deming Prize committee and its designated application prize subcommittee select the organizations that display the most meritorious application of the TQM principles. Each year in November, the winning organizations are awarded the Deming Prize in an elaborate ceremony.

Malcolm Baldrige National Quality Award

The Malcolm Baldrige National Quality Award was established in the United States by Public Law 100–107. The first awards were presented by President Ronald Reagan in November 1988. A copy of the application guidelines can be obtained from the U.S. Department of Commerce. In the 1989 guidelines' foreword, C. William Verity, secretary of commerce, states, "A strong quality system will benefit you and the Nation." It is reassuring to see the U.S. government promoting quality products and services.

Each year, up to two awards are presented in three categories. The categories are manufacturing or a subsidiary, service or a subsidiary, and small business. Whether or not a company fits into a category is determined by the standard industrial classification (SIC) codes. A small business is defined as an organization with more than 25 but fewer than 500 full-time employees. The organizations must be incorporated and located in the United States. May is the application deadline for the November awards.

The applications are reviewed and scored by a board of examiners. The board of examiners is comprised of quality experts from retired quality professionals, industry, professional and trade organizations, and universities. This initial scoring of the written applications will be used to select finalists. These finalists will then be subject to site visits by a team of examiners. Table 3.2 shows the examination categories used to score the various organizations.

A report of findings and a score are developed by the site visit team for submission to a nine-member panel of judges. The decision of the panel of judges is final. In order to minimize the effect of the individual site team's scoring bias, the site visit team leaders meet with the panel of judges to discuss the organizations and to regrade each one. Once this process is complete, the highest scoring organizations will be determined as the winners by the panel of judges. As previously mentioned, up to two awards per year per category can be awarded.

The application guidelines give a detailed description of each examination category and subcategory. The subcategories are broken down further into specific scoring criteria. A point value is assigned to each subcategory but not to each scoring criteria. Therefore, it is assumed each scoring criteria carries an equal weight.

Table 3.2: Examination categories for the 1993 Malcolm Baldrige National Quality Award.

Category	Points	Percent
1. Leadership	95	9.5
2. Information and analysis	75	7.5
3. Strategic quality planning	60	6
4. Human resource development and management	150	15
5. Management of process quality	140	14
6. Quality and operational results	180	18
7. Customer focus and satisfaction	300	30
Totals	**1000**	**100**

SUMMARY

Quality has drawn a tremendous amount of attention in recent years. Consequently, many organizations have developed measurement systems. Many states in the United States are now offering quality awards. In addition, there is now a British Quality Award. The Deming Prize and the Malcolm Baldrige National Quality Award are two of the most respected by quality professionals. Having worked at FPL since its adaptation of the TQM philosophy in 1981, I have a thorough understanding of the Deming Prize criteria as it pertains to a service organization. Thus, throughout the remainder of the text, I will use the Deming Prize measurement system to develop my theories. In no way am I implying the Malcolm Baldrige National Quality Award is second-class. The science of TQM is international and can be applied to any organization.

4
Policy Deployment

The first category in the JUSE Deming Prize checklist is policy deployment. Thus, the foundation of this text originates here. Once the procedure is developed, a case study is presented on how FPL has implemented policy deployment. In addition, a case study of SPATCO is presented. SPATCO is a small business that has undertaken the task of implementing policy deployment.

The objective of the policy process is to insure the organization attains its long-term plans. Thus, before an organization can develop an effective policy process, it must first have a vision and long-term management policies. The vision and long-term management policies, usually covering a 10-year horizon, are to be developed by the organization's senior management. It is advised that ownership of the policy deployment process throughout the organization be of utmost importance. Once the organization has a vision, it can develop a policy process to attain it. Table 4.1 outlines this process.

A policy organization needs to be in place to administer policy effectively. The following key functions are necessary.

President—appoints a senior management committee to oversee the policy process.

Senior management committee—develops long-term management policy. Appoints and oversees the policy committee. Approves annual policy. This committee has the ultimate responsibility to the customer.

Table 4.1: Policy process.

Assess customer's needs and reasonable expectations using
statistical quality control techniques to collect objective data.

↓

Top executives use this along with data from various areas of
expertise to develop the organization's strategy.

↓

This is set as the policy in the form of a vision and long-term,
mid-term, and short-term management policies.

↓

The policy is disseminated throughout the organization along
with a set of quantitative indicators and their respective targets.

↓

A single executive is assigned to oversee the analysis of a single
issue using statistical quality control techniques. Based on the
analysis, countermeasures are to be put in place.

↓

Effective countermeasures are to be standardized and replicated
whenever appropriate. An assessment of the results is made by
checking the indicators and targets.

↓

Finally, the entire policy process is assessed and improved as
needed. The process continues with the assessment of customer
needs and reasonable expectations.

Policy committee—conducts policy process.

Cross-functional committees—assess how well the organization is performing in the areas of quality, delivery, cost, safety, and morale. These committees are executive level, cross-functional.

Coordinating executive—develops plans to attain the goals of their assigned short-term management policy. This high-ranking executive is appointed by the policy committee to oversee one short-term (one to two years) management policy.

Functional managers—conduct projects to develop countermeasures. They work with the coordinating executive through win-win negotiations.

ESTABLISHMENT OF POLICY

The inputs necessary to establish policy are shown in Figure 4.1. Realistic policy is based on an assessment of economic conditions worldwide, factual data, personal knowledge of executives, and the organization's ultimate goal or vision. The policy established is to provide adequate guidance to the organization to achieve the vision. Based on the data, issues received by the various groups shown in Figure 4.1 and the existing policy (assuming this is not the first year policy is being set), the policy committee issues a draft policy to the senior management committee. It is to include the vision, long-term management policy, mid-term management policy, and short-term management policy. In addition, appropriate quantitative indicators and their respective targets are to be submitted. A clear support system to show how the draft policy supports the long-term management policy and vision is to be included. If approved, the president issues the draft policy to the organization. At this point, the draft policy is disseminated throughout the organization. Figures 4.2 and 4.3 show the entire process for both a large and small organization.

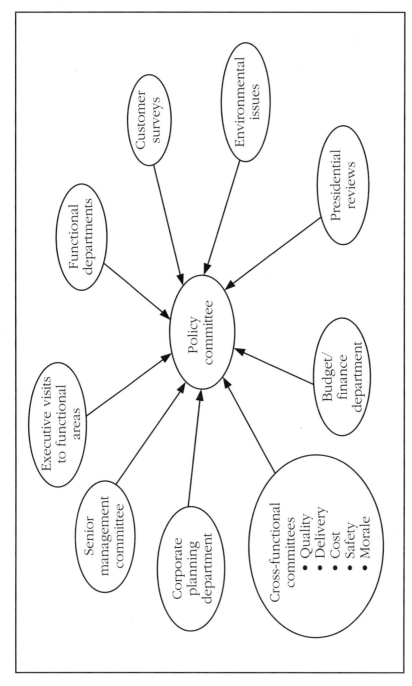

Figure 4.1: Inputs used to establish policy.

DISSEMINATION OF POLICY

For new short-term management policies, the policy committee is responsible for designating a coordinating executive. Existing short-term management policies already will have a coordinating executive. The coordinating executive is responsible for reviewing the validity of the short-term management policy, its quantitative indicator, and its respective target. If not acceptable, the coordinating executive establishes a dialogue with the policy committee to reach a consensus.

The coordinating executive will then assess, through the use of statistical quality control, where the organization currently is positioned concerning the short-term management policy. This information will be disseminated to functional areas within the organization that the coordinating executive designates as potential contributors. A full-day conference is scheduled between these designated functional areas and the coordinating executive. The functional managers determine where their departments are currently positioned regarding the short-term management policy prior to the full-day conference. At the full-day conference, the coordinating executive and functional managers will negotiate each functional area's contribution to meeting the short-term management policy's target. In a small organization, all the short-term management policies can be addressed in one conference.

Based on the input received during the conference, the coordinating executive assesses the corporation's ability to meet the short-term management policy's target. This is presented to the policy committee for approval. If not approved, the coordinating executive will hold another conference. Once approved, the organization will begin to analyze the short-term management policy.

At this point, the coordinating executive works closely with the functional managers to analyze the problem. The functional managers use statistical quality control techniques and employee teams to identify and verify the root causes. Once the root causes are known, countermeasures can be developed.

Two issues now must be addressed by the coordinating executive. First, are enough funds available to implement the countermeasures? If not, the funds need to be requested from the policy committee. Second, will the accumulated affect of the countermeasures meet the target? If not, either additional countermeasures are to be developed by the functional managers or the policy committee approves an adjustment of the target.

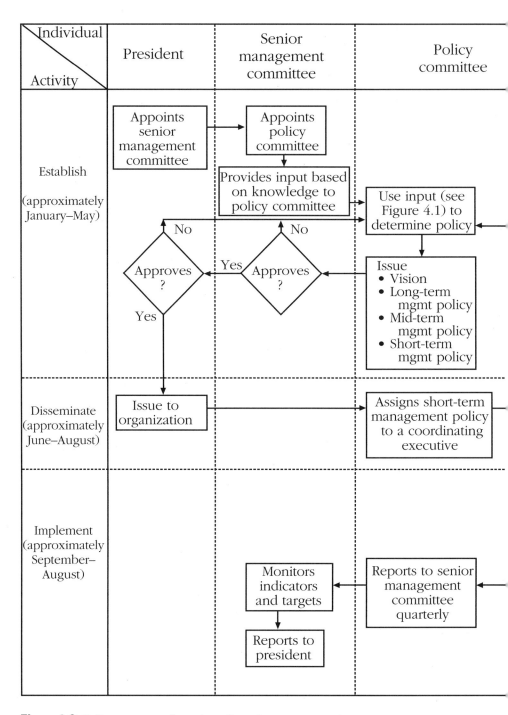

Figure 4.2: Policy process flowchart for a large corporation.

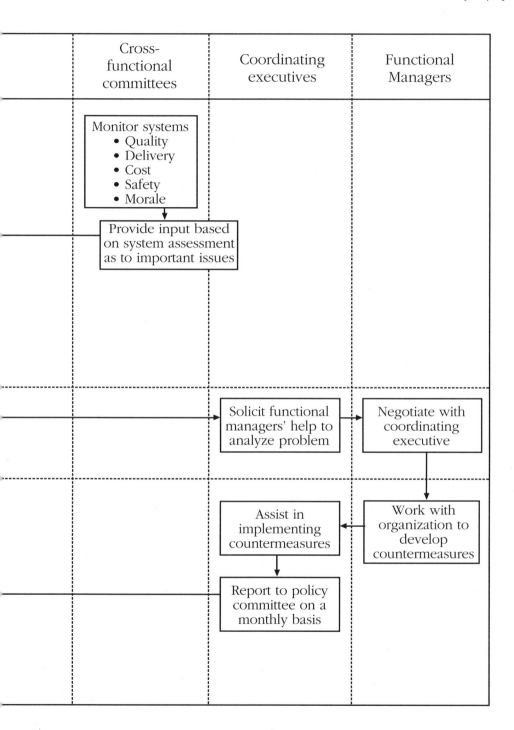

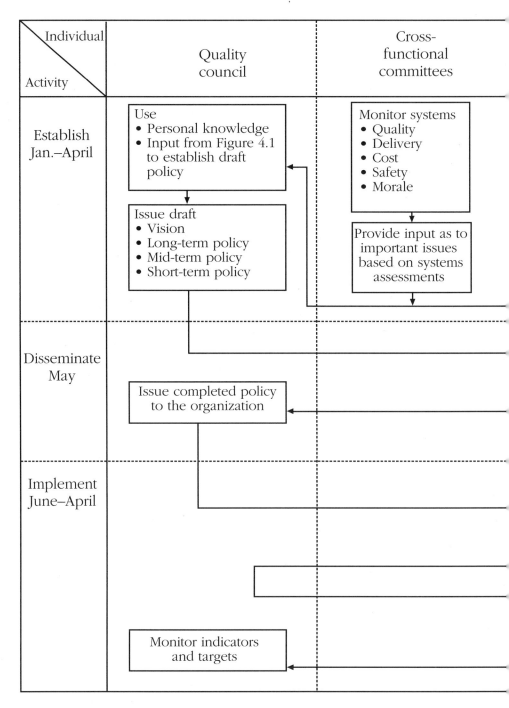

Figure 4.3: Policy process flowchart for a small corporation.

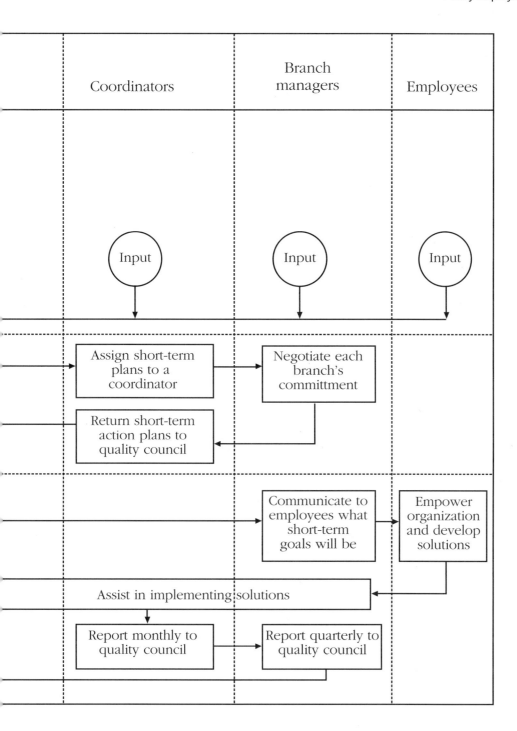

The policy committee will use this information to prepare the policy. The policy includes the vision, long-term management policies, mid-term management policies, and supporting short-term management policies, the countermeasures identified, and the quantitative indicators and targets. If the senior management committee approves it, the president will issue the policy to the organization. The organization then implements the policy.

IMPLEMENTATION OF POLICY

The functional managers, supervisors, and employees will implement the countermeasures they developed earlier in the process. In addition, employee teams can develop solutions throughout the year. On a monthly basis, the coordinating executive meets with the functional managers to assess their progress. If there are any discrepancies, corrective action is developed and implemented. The policy committee reviews the results and reports to the senior management committee quarterly. This review process includes a method for rewarding meritorious achievement as well as addressing inadequate achievement.

SUMMARY

The process concludes with the policy committee analyzing the policy process. Areas for improvement in the actual policy process are developed by the policy committee. In addition, suggestions from functional areas are reviewed by the policy committee and are implemented if approved.

The process outlined is conducted on a continuous basis, usually in annual cycles. As a short-term management policy is accomplished, it can be dropped from the policy. If the short-term management policy has not been achieved, and the policy committee feels it still warrants attention, it will remain in the policy. As the organization faces new challenges, new short-term management policies can be developed. Policy deployment is a continuous, flexible process to align the corporation in achieving its vision.

Large Corporation Case Study

The policy deployment process at FPL will be used as a case study of policy for a large corporation. FPL uses policy deployment to meet its customers' needs and reasonable expectations based on what FPL wants to provide as a product. The following is an overview of FPL's policy deployment.

Definition	Policy deployment is a management process to help achieve customer satisfaction through improvement objectives that support the corporate vision.
Purpose	To achieve breakthroughs by concentrating company efforts and resources on a few priority issues.
Benefits	Policy deployment improves intradepartmental communication, vertical and horizontal coordination and company participation in planning.[61]

Figure 5.1 shows FPL's management system.

The quality management system offers a systematic approach to prioritizing our accountabilities in response to customer needs. . . . The quality management system also shows the role we each have in fulfilling the primary objective of achieving customer satisfaction.

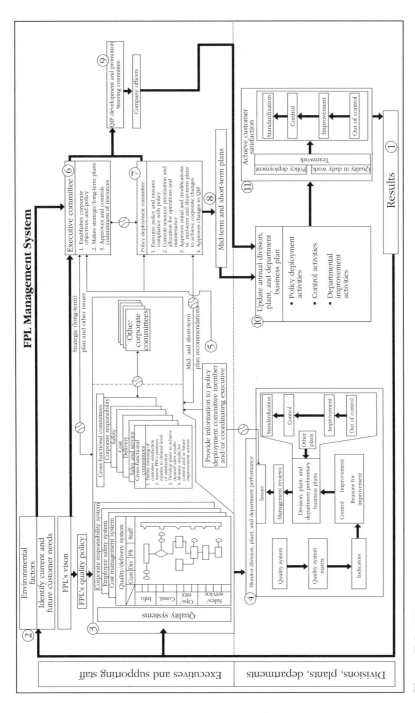

Figure 5.1: FPL's management system.

The quality management system may uncover high-priority issues, which because of their corporate nature, makes them prime candidates for policy deployment. Other priority issues are addressed by quality in daily work or quality improvement teams, using the quality improvement story process.[62]

The quality improvement story process is a problem-solving process that encourages the use of statistical quality control techniques. The key areas within FPL's policy deployment are as follows:

Policy Deployment Committee
The policy deployment committee is responsible to the executive committee for the policy deployment process. It is involved throughout all phases, most notably in developing guidelines, in evaluating and approving the proposed annual plan, in reviewing and reporting status of progress and finally in evaluating the results of the plan.

This committee also approves operating and maintenance budget requests, one of the preliminary steps to reviewing and submitting the final plan to the executive committee.[63]

Role of the Short-Term Coordinating Executive
This executive essentially becomes a project manager and assumes total responsibility for reviewing projects to insure they stay on schedule and on target. . . . The cross-functional nature of some steps in policy deployment calls for special cooperation between the coordinating executive and the functional areas targeted for support. This cooperation is vital, because of the key corporate improvements being sought. Conflicts in priorities should be resolved at the appropriate cross-functional level.[64]

Presidential Review
Here the coordinating executives and selected functional area managers present information on plans, systems of indicators, countermeasures and progress on short-term plans.[65]

Executive Visits

The data collected during individual executive visits is fed back and analyzed to help monitor company progress on its plans.

This check step also identifies potential problem areas for policy deployment attention by contributing to the analysis that starts the policy deployment process each year.[66]

Final Review: The Process Itself

To seek ways to improve policy deployment each year, FPL's chairman, president, and the policy deployment committee conduct an end-of-year assessment on the process and results.[67]

The evolution of FPL's management system is presented from their 1983's management by objectives (MBO) to 1990's draft policy deployment plans (Figures 5.2 through 5.10).

A summary of some of the results achieved through FPL's policy deployment process is presented in Table 5.1 on page 50.

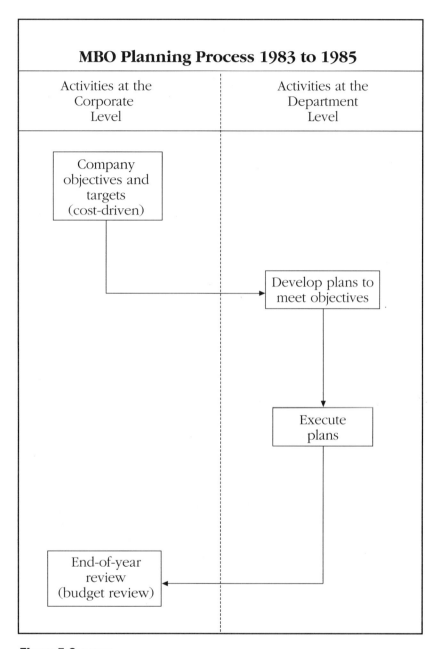

MBO Planning Process 1983 to 1985

Activities at the Corporate Level	Activities at the Department Level
Company objectives and targets (cost-driven)	Develop plans to meet objectives
	Execute plans
End-of-year review (budget review)	

Figure 5.2: MBO.

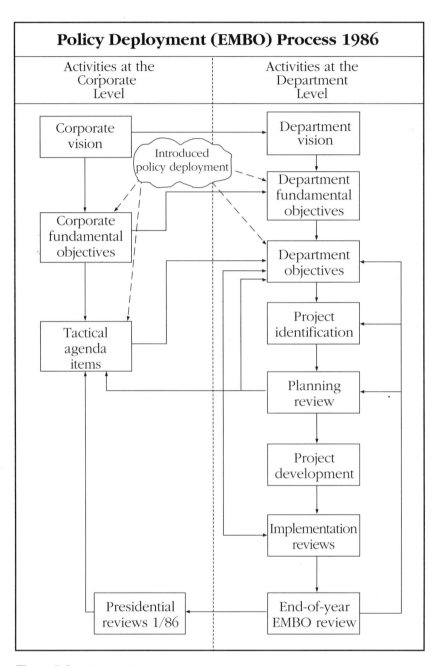

Figure 5.3: Enhanced MBO.

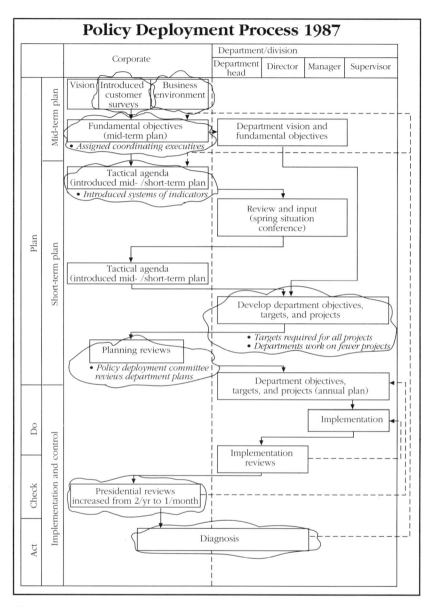

Figure 5.4: Policy deployment.

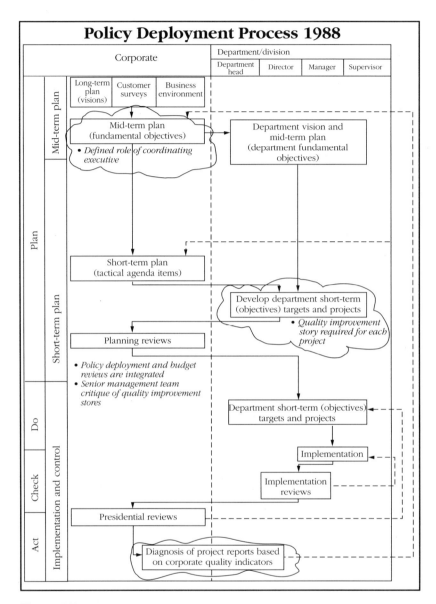

Figure 5.5: Policy deployment.

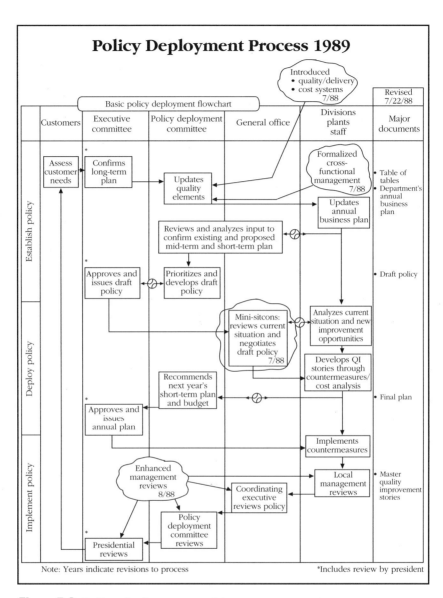

Figure 5.6: Policy deployment revisions.

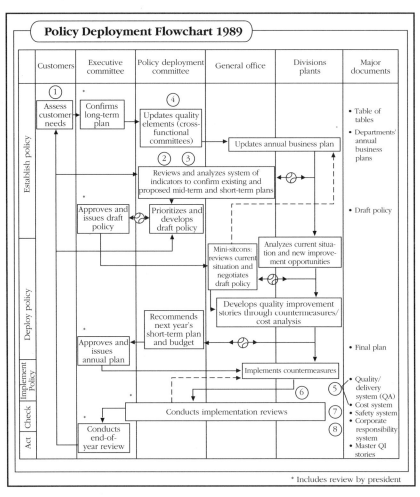

Figure 5.7: Policy deployment.

Policy Deployment Process Changes		
Year	Changes	Remaining Problems
Prior to 1985	**MBO**	• MBO objectives were only cost-related but not met—rate case (1984)
1985	**EMBO pilot** • Department planning reviews • Departments established vision, fundamental objectives, and departmental objectives • Focus more than cost • Establish policy deployment committee (cost/budget)	• Only three departments involved • No corporate level reviews • No end-of-year review to check on how well process worked
1986	**EMBO-corporatewide** • Establish presidential reviews • Establish end-of-year policy deployment review • Sitcon 4/86 focused on policy deployment/87 plan (mid-term and long-term plan)	• Great number of projects not completed (51.7%)-time of review November 1986 (16.5%)-not until 1987 • Too many projects—each department required to have projects for each short-term plan • No focus on corporate issues • No executive-level coordination
1987	**Policy deployment-corporatewide** • Customers point of view • Business environment considered • Departments established targets and indicators for projects • Guidelines revised to reflect reduction in number of projects—policy deployment guidelines (6/86) • Policy deployment committee met to review all projects 8/86 for 1987 • End-of-year review became diagnosis • Assigned coordinating executive to each short-term plan • Required quality improvement story format (for 88 plan)	• Only 46% of policy deployment targets met • Departments not aligning their priorities to corporate objectives (to achieve customer satisfaction)
1988	• Implemented management reviews (levels I, II, III) • Aligned short-term plans to corporate indicators for quality elements (quality systems) • Defined role of short-term plan coordinating executives • Required master quality improvement story format for control of short-term plan • Moved budget cycle to year end • Mini-sitcon coordinating executives now accountable to make targets • Formalized analysis from master quality improvement story reporting for each contribution	• 25% of targets not met • EFOR became unplanned for days off-line transmission forced outages • Nuclear energy equivalent availability • Short term plan 2.1 violations made overall, but Turkey Point failed • Alignment to quality elements off-cycle with table of tables update • Policy deployment actual versus target is too high
1989	• Formalized update procedure for table of tables to coincide with policy deployment calendar/policy deployment cycle • Established corporate format for "business plan" guidelines, standardized business plan process • Presidential review guidelines: –enhanced objectives to be more specific in the diagnosis of root cause (corporate level) –enhanced role of policy deployment committee to manage the action items from the meetings –formalized action item process • Introduced quality/delivery and cost systems • Formalized cross-functional management	

Figure 5.8: Policy deployment process changes.

Corporate Vision

During the next decade, we want to become the best managed electric utility in the United States and an excellent company overall and be recognized as such.

Quality elements	Element indicators	Short-term plans	1990 Policy deployment draft — Short-term indicators	Short-term plan 1990 target	Short-term plan 1992 target
Quality/delivery system					
Accurate answers/timely actions	Percent of calls with inaccurate answers				
	Percent of calls not answered in 48 seconds				
	Number of new meter set connected standards not met				
	Percent of construction jobs completed late				
Accurate bills	Meter reading errors per 1000 meters read				
	Inaccurate bills not processed by power billing				
	Percent of in-service meters tested outside required limits				
Considerate customer service	Number of Florida Public Service Commission complaints	1.3 Improve customer satisfaction	Number of customer complaints to the Florida Public Service Commission per 1000 customers	0.25	0.16
	Percent of calls with lack of caring (regional center-service observing)		Retain base sales of high load factor/high load customers	7424 Gigawatt Hours	7862 Gigawatt Hours
	Percent of calls with improper manner (regional center-service observing)				
	(Element indicator to be determined)				
Energy management assistance	Number of customers provided with energy management assistance				
Continuity of service	Service unavailability	1.1 Improve the reliability of electronic service	Distribution service unavailability	36.1 Customer minutes	31.8 Customer minutes
			Transmission service unavailability	To be determined customer minutes	To be determined customer minutes
			Substation service unavailability	To be determined customer minutes	To be determined customer minutes
Understandable rates/bills	Calls regarding understandable rates/bills				
Character of service	Number of Florida Public Service Commission complaints for voltage problems	4.2A Continue to emphasize safe, reliable, and efficient operation of nuclear power plants	Unplanned days off-line Turkey Point and St. Lucie	89	51
	Number of momentary interruptions				
Capacity	Summer peak reserve margin	4.3 Establish fossil unit reliability, availability, and maintainability targets, and develop a program that achieves those targets	Equivalent forced outage rate	4.88%	4.55%
	Loss of load probability				

Figure 5.9: Systems impact.

Quality elements	Element indicators	Short-term plans	1990 Policy deployment		
			Short-term indicators	Short-term plan 1990 target	Short-term plan 1992 target
Cost System					
Price	— Cents per Kilowatt Hour	4.1 Control price and provide competitive services through cost reductions and improved system utilization	— Operations and maintenance expenses	To be determined	To be determined
		4.2A Continue to emphasize safe, reliable, and efficient operation of nuclear power plants	— Unplanned days off-line (Turkey Point and St. Lucie)		
		4.3 Establish fossil unit reliability, availability, and maintainability targets, and develop a program that achieves those targets	— Equivalent forced outage rates		
	Rate options — Percent of small commercial/industrial customers on optional rates Percent of large commercial/industrial customers on optional rates Percent of residential customers on optional rates				
	Financial integrity — Debt ratio Pretax interest coverage ratio Return on common equity				
Corporate responsibility system					
	Prevent pollution/ protect public health — Number of environmental violations				
	Protect property and equipment — Indicator system to be held by vice president				
	Concern for community — Corporate contributions results Residential customer satisfaction survey results				
	Visual appeal — Residential customer satisfaction survey results				
	Protect natural environment — Number of natural resources environmental violations				
	Reporting and filing requirements — Percent of filing deadlines not met Percent of refiled documents				

Figure 5.9: Systems impact (continued).

Draft Policy Deployment Plan 1990

	Short-term plans	
Objectives	*Indicators*	
1.1 Improve the reliability of electric service	1.1A Distribution service unavailability (customer minutes)	
	1.1B Transmission service unavailability (customer minutes)	
	1.1C Substation service unavailability (customer minutes)	
1.3 Improve customer satisfaction	1.3A Number of customer complaints to the FPSC/1000 customers (excluding current division)	
	1.3B Retain base sales of high load factor/high load customers	
2.1 Strengthen FPL's effectiveness in dealing with special interest groups, governmental bodies, and regulatory agencies	2.1 Number of Nuclear Regulatory Commission violations— Turkey Point	
3.4 Improve employee safety	3.4 Number of lost time injuries per 100 FPL employees	
4.1 Control price and provide competitive services through cost reductions and improved system utilization	4.1 Operation and maintenance expenses ($ millions)	
4.2 Continue to emphasize safe, reliable, and efficient operation of nuclear power plants.	4.2A Unplanned days off-line (Turkey Point and St. Lucie)	
	4.2B Automatic trip rate—Turkey Point and St. Lucie (Trips per 1000 hours critical)	
4.3 Establish fossil unit reliability, availability, and maintainability targets and develop a program that achieves those targets.	4.3 Equivalent forced outage rate (%)	

Figure 5.10: Draft policy deployment plan.

CONFIDENTIAL

Targets 1990 1992	Quality categories				Coordinating executive
	Safety	Quality/delivery	Cost	Corporate responsibility	
	△	⊙	△		A. J. O.
	△	⊙	△		J. W. W.
	△	⊙	△		J. W. W.
		⊙	△		R. W. W.
		⊙	⊙		R. W. W.
	⊙	○	△	△	C. O. W.
	⊙	○	○		J. S. W.
			⊙		J. S. W.
		⊙	⊙		C. O. W.
	⊙	○			C. O. W.
		⊙	⊙		J. W. D.

⊙ High   ○ Medium   △ Low

Table 5.1: FPL's results.

Short-Term Plan	Indicator

Improve reliability of electric service	Customer minutes interrupted per customer served
	   1983 3/90
	78 minutes 44 minutes
	
	Number of unscheduled transmission outages
	   1985 12/89
	   950 660

Improve customer satisfaction	Florida Public Service Commission complaints per 1000 customers
	   1984 12/89
	   0.90 0.22

Improve employee safety	Lost time injuries per 100 FPL employees
	   1986 12/89
	   1.20 0.39

Control price and provide competitive services through cost reductions and improve system utilization	Total megawatt peak demand reduction capability
	   Started 12/89
	   in 1988 793 megawatts

Continue to emphasize safe, reliable, and efficient operation of nuclear power plants.	Automatic trips per 1000 hours of operation
	   1985 12/89
	   0.77 0.20

Establish fossil unit reliability, availability, and maintainability targets, and develop a program that achieves those targets	Equivalent forced outage rate
	   1987 12/89
	   14.0% 3.62%

6

Small Corporation Case Study

SPATCO will be used as a case study for a small corporation. SPATCO, a small corporation based in North Carolina, has three divisions: Petro Marketing Systems, Liquid Process Technology, and Environmental Services. The Petro Marketing Systems (Petro) division is primarily involved in distributing and servicing retailer petroleum equipment. SPATCO has had the Petro division since 1933. The Liquid Process Technology (LPT) division distributes pumps and process controls to organizations handling liquid. Chemical plants, the textile industry, and any industry moving liquid are LPT's primary customers. The LPT division was put in place at SPACTO in 1973. The last division, Environmental Services (ES), is SPATCO's youngest division. ES was started in 1987 to handle the influx of requests for environmental assistance.

SPATCO grew into three divisions through a natural evolution. SPATCO was a petroleum company familiar with pumps and tanks, and the liquid handling division was a natural progression. As customers from both the Petro and LPT divisions began asking SPATCO to provide assistance in the environmental area, a division to address these issues was formed.

SPATCO embraced TQM as a management system in January 1991. During January and February, the chief executive officer and the TQM director visited every branch and corporate office to introduce the employees to TQM. See Figure 6.1 for an overview of SPATCO's TQM process. In May 1991, SPATCO's management attended a three-day course to kick off its TQM efforts.

In developing the policy, it became apparent the rules of implementation at a large corporation could be modified. As a small corporation, SPATCO had fewer layers of formal management. This made it more agile and flexible.

The process began with SPATCO conducting research to determine the customers' needs and the employees' needs. Two studies were commissioned: a customer satisfaction survey and an employee attitude survey. In the history of SPATCO, these two tasks had never been performed on such a grand scale. The results of these two studies were used to determine the future direction of SPATCO. This direction was formally communicated to the organization through policy deployment.

The customer satisfaction survey asked the customers to rate SPATCO in 43 major areas. The 43 major areas were broken down into 10 categories.

1. Credibility
2. Quality
3. Reliability
4. Responsiveness
5. Communication
6. Understanding customer requirements
7. Price
8. Access
9. Courtesy
10. Tangibles

The customers were then asked to provide SPATCO with the score they would like to see a company in SPATCO's line of business receive. Thus, the gap between SPATCO's performance and what the customers expect assisted in setting the company's long-range direction.

SPATCO's employees were also asked to rate SPATCO's performance. This gap, the customers' perceptions of SPATCO's performance versus the employees' perceptions of SPATCO's performance, further enhanced the efforts to develop long-range plans. In addition, the employees were asked for input on how SPATCO could improve. Figure 6.2 shows a one-page summary of SPATCO's 1992 policy. Figures 6.3 through 6.6 show some of the indicators associated with SPATCO's short-term management policies. All 13 short-term management policies had a coordinator assigned to them. In addition, a quantitative measurement with targets for two years was developed for each short-term management policy.

SPATCO embraces TQM with the ultimate goal of making the customers, the employees, and the investors happy. Using policy deployment as a tool, SPATCO will align its human resources to move toward a common, beneficial set of goals. The desired result of policy deployment and TQM is total customer satisfaction. SPATCO is committed to total customer satisfaction, employee fulfillment, and financial success.

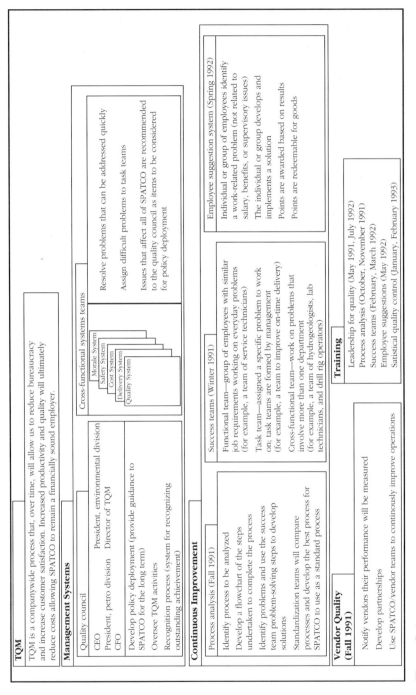

TQM

TQM is a companywide process that, over time, will allow us to reduce bureaucracy and increase customer satisfaction. Increased productivity and quality will ultimately reduce costs allowing SPATCO to remain a financially sound employer.

Management Systems

Quality council

CEO   President, environmental division
President, petro division   Director of TQM
CFO

Develop policy deployment (provide guidance to SPATCO for the long term)

Oversee TQM activities

Recognition process (system for recognizing outstanding achievement)

Cross-functional systems teams

Morale System
Safety System
Cost System
Delivery System
Quality System

Resolve problems that can be addressed quickly

Assign difficult problems to task teams

Issues that affect all of SPATCO are recommended to the quality council as items to be considered for policy deployment

Employee suggestion system (Spring 1992)

Individual or group of employees identify a work-related problem (not related to salary, benefits, or supervisory issues)

The individual or group develops and implements a solution

Points are awarded based on results

Points are redeemable for goods

Continuous Improvement

Process analysis (Fall 1991)

Identify process to be analyzed

Develop a flowchart of the steps undertaken to complete the process

Identify problems and use the success team problem-solving steps to develop solutions

Standardization teams will compare processes and develop the best process for SPATCO to use as a standard process

Success teams (Winter 1991)

Functional team—group of employees with similar job requirements working on everyday problems (for example, a team of service technicians)

Task team—assigned a specific problem to work on; task teams are formed by management (for example, a team to improve on-time delivery)

Cross-functional team—work on problems that involve more than one department (for example, a team of hydrogeologists, lab technicians, and drill rig operators)

Training

Leadership for quality (May 1991, July 1992)
Process analysis (October, November 1991)
Success teams (February, March 1992)
Employee suggestions (May 1992)
Satistical quality control (January, February 1993)

**Vendor Quality
(Fall 1991)**

Notify vendors their performance will be measured

Develop partnerships

Use SPATCO/vendor teams to continously improve operations

Figure 6.1: SPATCO's TQM process.

SPACTO ▼ POLICY 1992

Vision SPACTO is committed to total customer satisfaction, employee fulfillment, and financial success.

Long-term management policy 1992–2002	Mid-term management policy 1992–1997	Short-term management policy 1992–1993
1. Be the provider of choice for quality goods and services	1.1 Increase operational efficiency	1.1.1 Provide on-time delivery of products and services
		1.1.2 Reduce the number of vendor manufacturers
		1.1.3 Reduce the number of other vendors
	1.2 Conformance to valid requirements	1.2.1 Improve the ability of SPATCO to meet promised specs
	1.3 Provide responsive service to the customer	1.3.1 Provide a timely response to customer inquiries
	1.4 Offer a competitive price	1.4.1 Maintain profit levels that depict financial success
		1.4.2 Provide perceived value
2. Provide a superior work environment that empowers employees	2.1 Ensure employees are capable of performing their responsibilities	2.1.1 Provide employee training to enhance job performance
	2.2 Provide a safe work environment	2.2.1 Reduce the number of reportable accidents
3. Embody the highest ethical standards	3.1 Be credible in dealing with the customer	3.1.1 Provide credible, honest service to the customer
	3.2 Maintain open communications	3.2.1 Improve customer's perception of being informed
4. Contribute to our communities	4.1 Involve each operating unit in community activities	4.1.1 Be actively involved in each operating unit's community
5. Strive for continuous improvement	5.1 Assess every job function in the organization	5.1.1 Achieve continuous improvement through process analysis

Figure 6.2: SPATCO's policy.

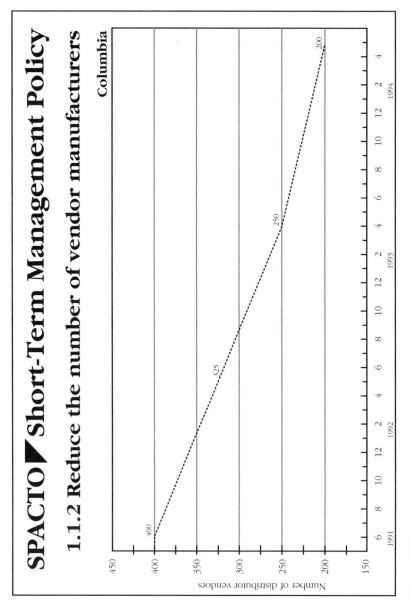

Figure 6.3: Reduce vendor manufacturers targets.

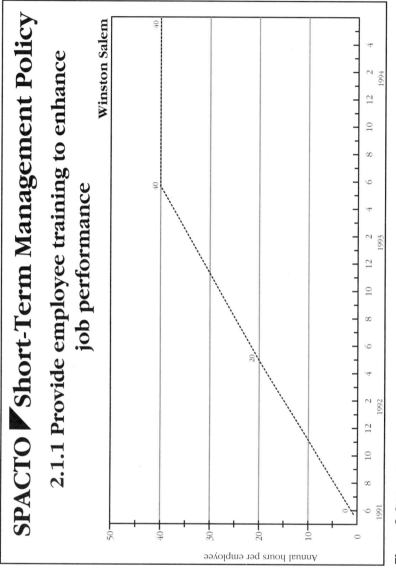

Figure 6.4: Employee training targets.

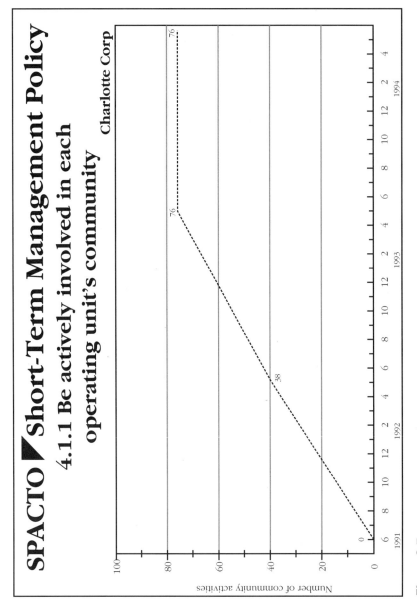

Figure 6.5: Community involvement targets.

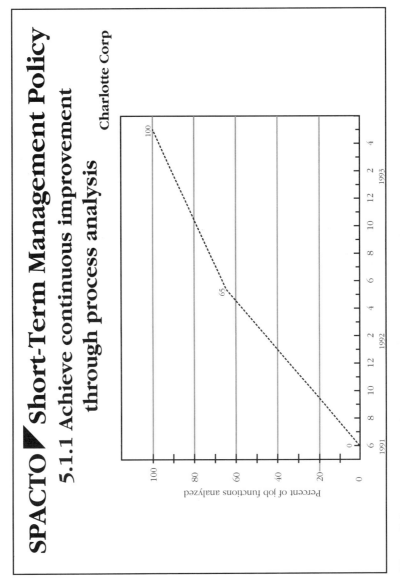

Figure 6.6: Process analysis targets.

7
What Next?
Japanese Approach to TQM

Previous chapters have developed a process to implement policy deployment, the first step in JUSE's Deming Prize criteria. What is next? An analysis of JUSE's TQM process is conducted by developing a checklist of the JUSE criteria for winning the Deming Application Prize based on an interpretation of Kansai Electric Company and working on FPL's TQM process for eight years. Logically following, in chapter 8, is a comparison of FPL's management services department to the checklist developed.

JUSE will not release the criteria it uses to measure Deming Prize applicants. However, JUSE publishes a checklist to use as a guideline in reviewing a TQM process. In addition to serving as a reviewing tool, these guidelines can also serve as a tool to implement a TQM process.

The Kansai Electric Company (1984 Deming Prize recipient and the first electric utility ever to win the award) has further broken down these guidelines for an electric utility. This information, along with my experience from working on FPL's TQM process for eight years, will be used as the basis for developing a guideline to review FPL's management services department. FPL was the first overseas company to have its application accepted for the Deming Application Prize for Overseas Companies in January 1989. Subsequently, FPL became the first overseas company to win the Deming Application Prize in November 1989. The guidelines developed herein will be used to determine how effectively an FPL department implemented TQM. The term *effective* is used confidently based on the recent performance of Japanese industry. Since 1951, JUSE has been awarding the Deming Application Prize to Japanese firms with the most meritorious TQM processes. Based on the quality products Japanese industry has been producing, this supports the use of the term *effective*.

To facilitate the case study of FPL's management services department, a checklist will be developed based on the Deming Prize's 10 subgroups of a TQM process. This checklist will serve as a guide for the case study. It is not intended to serve as a standard measurement for all TQM processes. As previously mentioned, each organization is different and each approach to TQM will be different. A checklist for a particular company or industry will be unique to that organization. However, an attempt is made to keep the checklist developed herein generic in nature.

According to the Deming Prize critera, there are 10 subgroups to be considered in the TQM process.

1. Policy
2. Organizational design
3. Education/training
4. Information
5. Analysis
6. Standardization
7. Control
8. Quality assurance
9. Effectiveness
10. Future plans

Kansai Electric Company dissected the 10 subgroups into various areas. The areas within each subgroup are outlined in the following pages. A subgroup is listed followed by the area within the subgroup. Each area is briefly described. Based on the area's description, an organization will decide how the area applies to its operations. A plan can then be developed to determine the amount of resources to be devoted to each area. Examples are spread throughout to support the application of selected areas.

7.1 POLICY

Areas within policy:
7.1.1 Policy for TQM Application

Develop a corporate principle or vision and disseminate it throughout the corporation. In addition, there are to be long-term (five to ten years), medium-term (two to five years), and short-term (one to two years) management policies set by the executive management of the organization. A system is to be in place to develop action plans for the management to implement these policies in the next year.

Define in writing what the corporation means by quality, quality control, quality assurance, total quality control, and so on. Explain the objectives of these various activities. Explain the budgetary process associated with TQM.

Example 7.1.1: FPL's Vision

During the next decade, we want to become the best managed electric utility in the United States and an excellent company overall and be recognized as such.

7.1.2 Process for Policy Establishment

A system is used to support the establishment of policy. What is the process, procedure, background, and philosophy for setting policy? The policy set is to be in support of the corporate principle/vision. A clear organization is in place defining the authority for the establishment of TQM policy.

7.1.3 Consistent and Realistic Policy

Policy is set based on a complete analysis of data. All policy is to be consistent throughout the organization. The short-term policy supports the medium-term policy that supports the organization's long-term policy. When establishing policy, consideration is to be equally distributed among costs, scheduling, human resources, product quality, and product quantity.

Realistic policy is based on an assessment of economic conditions worldwide, factual data, personal knowledge of executives, and the organization's ultimate goal or vision.

Example 7.1.3

FPL had a research, economics, and forecasting department that conducted extensive research concerning FPL's customers, regulatory requirements, and the economy. This information was vital to FPL setting clear direction.

7.1.4 Statistical Quality Control (SQC) Policy

An in-depth explanation of how SQC is being used in all sectors of the organization is to include the effectiveness and/or results obtained from the use of SQC.

What type of SQC instruction does the organization offer? Describe the competence of instructors, the course content, and the material used to supplement the instruction.

Example 7.1.4

In a service organization, SQC is not simply applied. Widgets are not popping off the end of an assembly line. However, FPL began extensive SQC training in its sixth year of implementing TQM. The course content ranged from lower level undergraduate to graduate level. When FPL first began implementing TQM, I never thought our employees would understand SQC. Much to my surprise, employees were applying and understanding control charts.

7.1.5 Policy Dissemination and Permeation

Management must disseminate the organization's policy, ensuring it permeates throughout. A feedback loop needs to be in place so that the organization receives and understands the policy. A flowchart of this process is recommended. The evolution of this process will lead the organization to achieve its objective or vision from the support of the annual, mid-term, and long-term objectives.

Example 7.1.5

At SPATCO, all employees were introduced to policy deployment personally by members of the quality council.

7.1.6 Implementation of Policy to Achieve the Organization's Goals

Did the policy provide adequate guidance to the organization to acheive its vision or goal? Through the evolution of the management policy, what has been accomplished? Once this has been determined, a plan for dealing with weaknesses needs to be developed. This should include a method for rewarding meritorious achievement as well as addressing inadequate achievement.

7.1.7 Relationship Between Long-Term and Short-Term Policies

A philosophy for developing long-term policy needs to be established. In addition, a philosophy for short-term policy and its relationship to the long-term policy should be developed. This philosophy should include a method for revising policy. Policy revision may be necessary in case of meritorious/inadequate achievement, new technology, a change in economic conditions, and so on.

Example 7.1.7

It is important not to change targets without an explanation. In other words, targets should not be adjusted just because the organization had difficulty achieving them.

7.2 ORGANIZATIONAL DESIGN

Areas within organizational design:
7.2.1 Assignment of Responsibility and Authority
Develop organizational charts for the entire organization. Definitions for the individual department's function, responsibility, and level of authority are necessary. A written procedure to cover the development of the organizational charts should be provided to the departments clearly specifying who approves the organizational charts. In addition, the individual responsibilities for TQM implementation should be included on the organizational charts.

7.2.2 Delegation of Authority
Establish a procedure to determine who has the authority to delegate and what they can and cannot delegate. The procedure should provide practical examples. In addition, corrective action by management when a delinquency or weakness occurs should be described. Finally, management will audit this area to improve quality assurance and quality control.

> *Example 7.2.2*
> The power of having an organization chart becomes apparent once one is developed. Employees may not agree with it, but once a chart is developed there is no question where everyone fits. This simple tool was very effective at FPL.

7.2.3 Interdepartmental Cooperation
A formal system should be in place explaining the process for horizontal and vertical communication between departments. In addition, it should be described how each department communicates with the TQM department, and documentation should be provided to show the effectiveness of these interactions.

7.2.4 Corporate Committees
Define the different committees within the organization. Provide justification for the establishment of these committees. Does the committee have the authority to implement its responsibilities? Provide an example of a committee that has attained remarkable achievement.

> *Example 7.2.4*
> FPL's safety committee reduced lost time injuries per 100 employees from 1.20 in 1986 to 0.39 in December 1989. This is an incredible 68 percent improvement.

7.2.5 Staff

Explain policy used to manage staff positions. How are staff positions assigned and what policy is used? Explain how human resources are recruited to perform these tasks. How are staff trained generally and for specialized tasks? Provide details for long-term training.

A procedure should be in place to provide training for successors. How does staff improve management efficiency? What is the policy for the action taken for unqualified personnel? How is employee effectiveness measured? What is the contribution of the TQM department staff with respect to each committee, project, or group activity? Finally, give an example of the job description of a staff position.

7.2.6 Quality Control (QC) Circle Activities

Describe how management administers and tracks the progress and results of their QC circles. Is there a manual and course for the QC circles? Explain how QC circles are promoted and given guidance. Is there a success and/or failure example of QC circles?

Example 7.2.6

At one point in time, FPL had over 1000 QC circles. One St. Lucie Nuclear Plant team reduced outage time saving FPL millions of dollars.

7.2.7 Quality Control Diagnosis

Provide a flowchart showing how management performs a diagnosis of the organization. How is management trained for this task? Explain how the diagnosis takes place. Provide documentation showing action items, the priority management gave to these action items, and the results achieved. Show how management is improving the diagnosis process.

7.3 EDUCATION/TRAINING

Area within education/training:
7.3.1 Education Plan

The organization should have an education policy. How are the needs for training evaluated? Explain the budget and facilities used for training. How are the instructors graded (provide test scores)? How are the participants graded (provide test scores)? Provide data and schedules on courses held.

Example 7.3.1
FPL's organizational development and training department was an exceptional education resource. Team courses, SQC, and management courses were designed and administered by FPL employees. Instructors and students received pre- and post-testing.

7.3.2 TQM Awareness
Explain procedures used to evaluate employees understanding of TQM. How are action plans developed to correct discrepancies? Explain how textbooks for courses are evaluated and updated.

7.3.3 SQC Education
Explain how participants are selected for SQC courses. What are their test scores before and after attending the SQC course? How is the participant's application of the SQC techniques monitored? Describe the procedure for qualifying instructors.

Example 7.3.3
In one of FPL's SQC courses, the participant must complete an SQC project in his or her workplace. Over a four-month period, the participant presents a monthly progress report to a senior management review committee. The participant must apply SQC techniques successfully before graduating from the course.

7.3.4 Education Effectiveness
Provide procedures used to measure education effectiveness along with supportive documentation. How do the actual results compare to the expected results? Describe the most effective and least effective courses. Have any refresher courses been implemented? What changes have been made as a result of the course evaluations?

Example 7.3.4
FPL found that team leaders needed more training after four or five years. A team leader refresher course was developed to update employees who previously had taken the team leader course.

7.3.5 Supplier Education/Training
What type of TQM training is given to suppliers? How is the effectiveness evaluated? What type of corrective action has resulted from supplier evaluation?

Example 7.3.5
FPL began reviewing and educating vendors through its vendor quality improvement program (VQIP).

7.3.6 Education for QC Circles
Explain programs available to train QC circle leaders and facilitators/promoters. How is the effectiveness of the courses measured? Provide statistics to support the findings. How are instructors qualified? Explain on-the-job training for QC circle leaders and facilitators.

7.3.7 Suggestion System
Provide a description of the suggestion system. Provide up-to-date statistics for the program. Explain the organization in place to administer and promote the suggestion system. Document how suggestions are evaluated.

Example 7.3.7
In one year, FPL went from receiving 200 to 300 suggestions to over 35,000 suggestions annually.

7.4 INFORMATION

Areas within information:
7.4.1 Collection of External Information
Explain policy for collecting, summarizing, analyzing, transmitting, and evaluating external information. Explain policy for distributing TQM-related information and the corresponding feedback mechanism. Provide a detailed list of the external indicators that are monitored. Are any indicators of your competitors monitored? Is there an example where the information collected has benefitted the organization significantly?

7.4.2 Intercommunication of Information
Explain the procedure used to communicate information within the organization. How is the information to be communicated selected, and what types of benefits are hoped to be achieved? How do you ensure that information reaches its destination? How is confidential information handled?

7.4.3 Timeliness of Information
Are any process flow systems in place to show the timely transmission

of data? How is the information concerning customers transmitted? Have problems occurred due to late information? If so, show the improved process flow system to correct these problems. Explain the use of computers for information transmission. Provide the best example of the benefits of timely information transmission.

7.4.4 Information Utilization

Explain the procedure used to analyze information. What statistical methods are used? How do you know the end user of the information is satisfied? What actions are being taken to improve the analysis of information? What type of systems are used for the storage and retrieval of information?

> *Example 7.4.4*
>
> FPL's research, economics, and forecasting department produced what it called the table of tables. It provided pertinent information to the organization. Unfortunately, it took many employees years to figure out how to read the table of tables.

7.5 ANALYSIS

Areas within analysis:
7.5.1 Improvement Opportunity Selection

Explain the process used for selecting critical problems. How are facts analyzed and presented? Explain the process used to determine the priority of the critical problems. How are themes established and supporting indicators selected? How are themes and indicators authorized? Explain the process for determining the reliability and traceability of the data sources.

7.5.2 Process of Analysis

How is the most appropriate method of analysis determined? How are the QC tools used justified? Who is responsible for determining the method of analysis? Explain the link between the analysis and the conclusions drawn. Have any new analysis techniques for common problems been discovered?

> *Example 7.5.2*
>
> Quite often, FPL employees struggled with selecting the proper tools to use for analysis. This pain is a real element of the TQM journey. It took time, but employees were much more capable of solving problems because of struggling with analysis techniques.

7.5.3 Use of SQC

Discuss what SQC methods are used. Which SQC methods are used most frequently and why? Has it been determined if engineers are using SQC methods? Provide an example. Have breakthroughs been achieved through the use of SQC? What actions are being taken to improve the use of SQC methods?

7.5.4 Analysis Within Organization

Explain if any difficulty was experienced in analyzing any specific areas within the organization. Explain the cause of the difficulty. Show verification that the root cause of the difficulty was determined and addressed. What type of statistical analysis was used to solve the problem? Give an example. How many problems are solved using statistical analysis? What type of problems remain in the organization, and what type of statistical analysis can be used to eliminate them?

> *Example 7.5.4*
>
> Employees in FPL's trouble department analyzed the process to respond to customers' electric power supplies being interrupted. Many techniques were used including control charts. The analysis reflected that in extreme cases (outside three standard deviations) the customer's power could be out for over 12 hours. In 1983, customers were interrupted an average of 78 minutes per year, in March 1990, it was 44 minutes. This represented a 44 percent reduction in outage time.

7.5.5 Quality and Process Analysis

Explain analysis techniques used to determine the quality of products and services. How is this verified through the customers? What problems are encountered in analyzing quality? What action is being taken to eliminate these problems? What benefits are obtained from quality analysis?

Explain the procedure used to decide when to apply process analysis. How is process analysis conducted? Explain process capability measuring procedures. Who is responsible for process analysis procedures? What actions are taken when a weakness in a process is identified? Explain the benefits achieved through process analysis and its use in standardization.

7.5.6 Use of Analysis Results

Is there a procedure explaining how to transfer analysis into effective countermeasures? Give examples of remedial corrective actions and recurrent preventive actions based on analysis results. If available, show how these actions were standardized and replicated throughout the organization.

Example 7.5.6

On several occasions, the results obtained by FPL teams were so impressive, FPL applied for patents. A group had to be formed to handle patent requests due to the high volume of good ideas.

7.5.7 Encouragement of Continued Results

Is there a formal process for submitting the methodology used and results obtained to the organization? How are these suggestions evaluated by management? Show how the submission and evaluation processes are being improved.

Example 7.5.7

FPL had a formal quality improvement story procedure. It was a standardized method of telling a story. Each story was submitted to information central, an internal record-keeping department.

7.6 STANDARDIZATION

Areas within standardization:

7.6.1 Standardization System

Show the company's policy and organizational chart associated with the standardization system. How does the standardization system provide standards for all the organization's departments (quality control, engineering, production, and so on)? Show how the standardization system issues new standards, educates the work force, and provides support to the departments. Give an assessment of the standardization system.

7.6.2 Establishment, Revision, and Rescission Procedures

Explain the procedures in place for the establishment, revision and rescission of company procedures. Is a central location responsible? Who is responsible for approving standard changes? Show an example of a procedure and explain the steps involved with it.

Example 7.6.2

FPL had a procedures department that handled the establishment, revision, and rescission of standards.

7.6.3 Status of Establishment, Revision, and Rescission Procedures

Explain the process by which a newly established procedure is developed and eventually arrives in the user's possession. Are there any establishment process indicators? How long does it take for a procedure to be revised? Show indicators. Explain the process used to recover old procedures. Explain the process to rescind a procedure. How do you guarantee that a rescinded procedure is not followed by the user?

7.6.4 Content of Standards

Explain how the standards are developed so that the user can understand and implement them. How do you measure customer satisfaction for the standards? Is a process in place to review standards periodically to ensure that their contents are meaningful in the present? Are standards ever revised due to a line employee's suggestions? If so, how often does this occur?

> *Example 7.6.4*
> Standards at FPL were primarily written by the employees. Changes to standards were reviewed by departments throughout FPL and, if approved, were made. Many changes were the result of TQM activities.

7.6.5 Use of Statistical Methods

Explain how statistical methods are used during the establishment, revision, or rescission of a procedure. How many technical and engineering standards are supported by a statistical analysis? Is statistical analysis consulting available to groups working on company procedures?

> *Example 7.6.5*
> FPL's quality improvement department had several competent individuals on its staff available as statistical analysis consultants.

7.6.6 Technology Accumulation

Explain the process used to accumulate and distribute technology effectively. Is this technology used to reevaluate standards? Explain how technology accumulation is handled for the various departments within the organization. Who is responsible for technology accumulation? Show a case study of an adopted technology and explain how it was replicated. Has the organization developed any original research resulting in new technology?

Example 7.6.6

Several staff groups were responsible for new technology accumulation. Surprisingly, the FPL employees in the field began creating their own rules. One team developed a pole top mounted rig to help crews pull wire. A team member welded a prototype at home in his garage. (FPL applied for a patent.)

7.6.7 Use of Standards

Explain how the organization monitors the use of standards. Has nonconformance to standards ever been measured? What is the risk to the organization and the effect on the customer due to nonconformance? Give an example of an effective standard.

Example 7.6.7

FPL's internal auditing department audited conformance to standards. In addition, engineering and construction were audited randomly. Finally, customer calls were monitored randomly by telephone board supervision.

7.7 CONTROL

Areas within control
7.7.1 Control System for Quality

What type of control systems are used to manage the organization and its various functions? Are the systems on a flowchart? Is there a written procedure? Are the organizational control systems correlated to the functional control systems? Separate control systems on an organizational level are required for quality, cost, delivery, safety, and morale. On a functional level, all of the systems mentioned above, with the addition of a human resources system, are required. Explain the process for dealing with an out-of-control system. Show an example of how you resolved an out-of-control system condition. How do individual employees relate to the systems mentioned above?

Example 7.7.1

At SPATCO, cross-functional teams consisting of employees from all levels of the company address quality, cost, delivery, safety, and morale. These teams meet once every two months to address issues in their area.

7.7.2 Control Points and Control Items

Define control points and control items. Explain the process management uses to determine control points and control items based on the control system for quality (section 7.7.1). Give an example of one manager's control points and control items. What is the status of this manager's control points and control items?

7.7.3 Use of Statistical Methods

Define how statistical methods are used throughout the development of control systems for quality. Are control charts used? Are other statistical methods used? Explain how the statistical methods used to develop control systems for quality are disseminated to the individual employees. Give an example of how the use of statistical methods contributed to a remarkable change.

7.7.4 Contribution of QC Circles

Explain how QC circles implement the plan-do-check-act concept of quality control. How do QC circles contribute to the improvement of the control system for quality? Give an example of how a QC circle prevented an out-of-control situation. What is the current status of the QC circles supporting the control system for quality?

> *Example 7.7.4*
> SPATCO's control system has the authority to appoint task teams to address out-of-control situations.

7.7.5 Status of Control Systems

Explain the procedure used to review the various control systems. What format is used to report the status of the control systems? How often is an evaluation of the control systems conducted? What is the involvement of the top executives? Give an example of the action taken when an abnormal condition was discovered.

> *Example 7.7.5*
> At SPATCO, the cross-functional control system teams report to the quality council. All expenditures required are approved by the quality council. A 15-minute review is given after each team's bimonthly all-day meeting.

7.7.6 Steady-State Condition

Graphically show control points or control items that are operating under control. Explain how the control limits are set and who approves them. Explain the process used to address out-of-control systems. Give an example of the actions taken to resolve an out-of-control system. Once a steady state is reached, what is the plan of action for further improvement?

7.8 QUALITY ASSURANCE

Areas within quality assurance:
7.8.1 New Product Development

What is top management's quality assurance policy for new product development? Is there a new product development procedure? If so, who is responsible for it, and what are the long-term plans for new product development? Has a national organization been formed to support new product development within the industry? If so, what is the corporation's involvement? How is information on new product development throughout the industry collected and evaluated? Explain how the above information is used to develop new product policy.

The following information should be available for new products.

- Prediction of sales volume
- Level of quality
- Estimated price
- Prediction of production costs
- Date of opening sale
- Estimation of quantity to produce
- Prediction of life cycle costs
- Service strategy
- Locations where product will be sold
- Sales strategy
- Training and education needs

Show how statistics are used, based on the information above, to determine the technological feasibility, process capability, and resource availability to produce the new product.

7.8.2 Quality Evolution, Quality Analysis, Reliability, and Design Review

Explain the procedure in place to ensure quality evolution and analysis. Give examples of how this procedure has been used to improve quality as perceived by the customer.

Discuss the reliability control system in place, its organization, and any procedures developed. How does the reliability group review new product development, customer claims, and product failure? What type of reliability training is conducted? What is the reliability status by product, and how does this relate to customer satisfaction?

Explain the design review systems and procedures. Explain in detail how the design review of a product or service is conducted. Are practices established and manuals developed to evaluate product design and to ensure customer satisfaction? What qualifications do the design engineers have, and how is this level of education maintained? Explain the procedure used to test and change the design. Explain how the objectives of a test are developed and how the results of the testing are disseminated. Give an overview of the testing facilities available, the funds budgeted for testing, and the process used to evaluate test results.

Example 7.8.2

FPL offers an undergraduate-level reliability course. Several employees addressing customer's power supply interruption applied the reliability analysis techniques. A history of reliability data by equipment type was used to direct team efforts. This analysis separated the vital few from the trivial many and allowed limited resources to be used effectively.

7.8.3 Safety and Product Liability Prevention

Define the safety program and its organization and procedures. How many employees are involved in carrying out safety? How are these employees trained? Explain the corporation's viewpoint on the cost of safety versus the quality, cost, and delivery of the product. What are the future plans to improve safety?

Explain company policy regarding product liability. What types of lawsuits has the organization suffered due to product liability? Explain the system in place to handle casualties and to disseminate this information to top executives. Explain how product liability is incorporated into the design of products.

7.8.4 In-Process Control

Define in-process control procedures. How is quality assurance of in-process material maintained? Explain how in-process material is stored, transported, and measured once in the system. Explain how equipment, tools, and vehicles are maintained. How do QC circles contribute to improved in-process control? What are the consequences of inadequate in-process control?

7.8.5 Process Capability

Explain the process capability system in place. How is it used to measure each process? Is this information used to set goals? How is feedback of process capability disseminated throughout the organization? What is the current status of each process capability measurement? What type of education is conducted on the concepts of process capability?

> *Example 7.8.5*
>
> As part of SQC training, FPL taught process capability. (The trouble office team used it on service interruption control charts.)

7.8.6 Measurement and Inspection

Explain organization in place and procedures available for the measurement and inspection functions. Describe the instruments, tools, gages, and test equipment used for measurement. Explain how calibration and tolerance levels are determined and set. Describe the purchasing procedure for measurement equipment with particular attention on how quality is assured. Describe the process used to qualify inspectors. What type of certification is required by law, regulations, or internal requirements? Explain how reliability, maintainability, and safety are incorporated into the inspection process. Describe the process used to determine when inspection occurs. How are nonconforming products dealt with? What type of records are kept, and how is this data used for life cycle costing and new product design? Explain how cooperation is maintained between inspection and production personnel.

> *Example 7.8.6*
>
> At FPL, an exceptional amount of measurement occurred in the nuclear side of the business. In the distribution side of the business, the following is an example of some of the measurements.
>
> • Voltage dip or surge
> • Line current
> • Number of breaker trips
> • Customer minutes interrupted
>
> In addition, FPL has a testing facility where equipment is tested until failure under various conditions.

7.8.7 Equipment, Vendor, Subcontractor, and Service Control

Describe the equipment maintenance control system, organization, and procedures. Explain the philosophy regarding basic and preventive maintenance. How is equipment failure and unsatisfactory performance monitored? How are these data used to determine future procurement? Explain how new technology is evaluated and incorporated into new equipment purchases.

Define the organization's procurement policy. Regarding suppliers, how are the following areas evaluated?

- Quality control
- Quality assurance
- Production control
- Cost control
- Training and education programs
- Conformance to specifications, and so on

What type of indicators are monitored? How often are vendors' locations inspected? Are vendors required to have a TQM process? If so, what assistance is provided? How often are vendors' top executives invited to visit the organization?

Describe the procedures in place to furnish customer service and describe the organization in place to carry out this function. Are service systems in place before new products are released? In other words, are repair manuals/equipment/parts available? Are customer service personnel trained? Are warranty policies clearly explained? Explain how customers are surveyed for their satisfaction level and how the results are used for new product design. Describe qualifications necessary to be customer service representatives. What type of training are they provided?

Example 7.8.7

FPL used a cable failure report (CFR) to track the failure of cable under actual field conditions. This information was used by its engineering department and was shared with FPL's vendors. When the circumstances called for it, the actual piece of failed cable was further analyzed at FPL's test lab to help determine the root cause of the failure.

7.8.8 Quality Assurance System and Its Diagnosis

Describe how the organization assures quality in the following areas:
- Market analysis
- Planning

- Design
- Trial production
- Post-trial design
- Post-trial production
- Inspection
- Sales
- Service
- Disposal

What type of diagnostic systems are in place to monitor quality assurance at each phase? How effective are the diagnostic systems? Give an example.

7.8.9 Use of Statistical Methods

Give examples of how statistical methods are being used in the quality assurance area. What is being done to educate the organization in using statistical methods for quality assurance?

Example 7.8.9

One topic of importance to note here is FPL's employees use of SQC to understand when data are significantly different. In other words, were the circumstances due to a special situation or were they common within the current process? Getting employees to understand the difference between special causes and common causes was a major contribution of SQC.

7.8.10 Quality Evaluation and Quality Audit

Define the organization's quality evaluation and quality audit procedures. How is quality evaluated? What organization is responsible for its evaluation and what authority does it have? How are quality audits conducted? Who uses the results of the quality audits? How does the quality control department use audit information? What type of feedback is provided to the audited group?

Example 7.8.10

Extensive audits were performed internally by FPL management. In addition, JUSE counselors performed periodic third-party quality audits.

7.8.11 Status of Quality Assurance

Explain how each department's quality assurance activities align with corporate policy. How is ongoing product quality assured? Are products periodically evaluated for customer satisfaction while customers are using the products? How are products compared to competitor's products to ensure quality, reliability, availability, and so on?

Example 7.8.11

At FPL, the annual business plan addressed these issues.

7.9 EFFECTIVENESS

Areas within effectiveness:

7.9.1 Measurement of Effectiveness

Explain the procedures for measuring the effectiveness of the TQM process. Who is responsible for monitoring the TQM process? Give an example of some of the indicators used. How are the results of measurement used to determine future policy?

Example 7.9.1

FPL did an excellent job using quantitative quality indicators (see Table 5.1 on page 50).

7.9.2 Tangible Effectiveness

Using quantitative data, show how improvement has been achieved in the following areas:

- Quality
- Service
- Delivery
- Cost
- Profit
- Safety
- Environment
- Other valid areas

Example 7.9.2

In the area of service, FPL had 0.90 complaints per 1000 customers in 1984 and 0.22 in December 1989. The definition of the indicator was complaints received by the Florida Public Service Commission per 1000 customers. This improvement represented a 76 percent decrease in customer complaints.

7.9.3 Intangible Benefits

Describe how employees' attitudes have changed. How is the organization enhancing management by policy deployment? Are employees submitting more improvement suggestions? What has been the trend of intangible benefits over the previous five years?

Example 7.9.3

FPL employees will never address a problem in the same manner after their exposure to TQM. A team of five meter readers in suits and ties presented their quality improvement story to the division vice president and his lead team. Upon completion, one of the team members said, "In my wildest dreams, I never thought the division vice president would listen to anything I had to say."

7.9.4 Predicted Versus Actual Results

Explain the process used to predict corporate goals. How often are the predictions revisited and reevaluated? Are the predicted results being achieved? If not, what actions have been taken? Give examples.

Example 7.9.4

At FPL and SPATCO, all the corporate indicators had quantitative targets. Actual numbers were compared to the targets. This gave the organization clear feedback on its efforts.

7.10 FUTURE PLANS

Areas within future plans:
7.10.1 Current Situation

Support with data, if available, the present status of the organization. Define the most crucial issues facing the organization. Have these issues been addressed? If so, have they been resolved? Show an example of an issue that has been resolved.

7.10.2 Planning for Critical Issues

Explain the process used to identify the causes of these critical issues. Are corrective actions planned to address these issues? Show the status of implementing these corrective actions.

7.10.3 Future Planning

Explain the process the organization has in place to anticipate future critical issues. How is prevention of the issues dealt with? Are these issues reflected in the corporation's policy deployment plan?

7.10.4 Relationship with Long-Term Planning

Describe the link between future planning (section 7.10.3) and the development of long-term plans. What process is in place to monitor this relationship, and who is responsible for it?

Example 7.10.4

FPL went into shock when asked to plan beyond one year. Through its TQM efforts, departments are now concerned with 5- to 10-year horizons. As indicative of FPL's vision, the corporation is moving toward a 10-year-plus horizon.

SUMMARY

The checklist developed in this chapter contains the formula many Japanese organizations have used to become producers of quality products and services. Any organization can use this checklist to build an effective TQM process. If an area is not understood clearly, seek professional assistance.

8

Ten-Step Case Study

This case study will be based on FPL's management services department, the internal industrial engineering consulting department of a large service corporation.

Most of the information provided by FPL was extracted from the management services department's 1990 business plan. The business plan is a tool management services used to organize its TQM activities. Chapter 7 outlined the 10 subgroups to be considered in the TQM process (see page 62).

The following is a review of FPL's management services implementation of the TQM process. Figure 8.1 illustrates management services' link to *policy deployment* (item 1). The short-term plans were part of FPL's policy. Many of the projects undertaken by the management services group directly or indirectly assisted FPL in meeting these short-term plans.

Figures 8.2 and 8.3 outline the *organizational design* (item 2). Figure 8.2 provides a broad view while Figure 8.3 provides a detailed view of the department's organizational design. A clear structure is communicated to the employees, the rest of the corporation, the customer, and anyone interested in understanding the department.

Just for a moment, imagine visiting FPL's management services department. Suppose a two-hour meeting had been scheduled to discuss new computer software. How much more productive could the meeting be if Figures 8.2 and 8.3 were distributed in advance?

Figure 8.4 provides a detailed review of *education/training* (item 3). The management services department developed a process to determine the education/training needs of the individuals within the department, to assess the best method to acquire this training, and to develop an action plan to achieve its goals. This process includes the evaluation of in-house FPL training and courses offered through conferences, seminars, universities, and so on.

Included in Figures 8.5, 8.6, and 8.7 are the subgroups of *information* (item 4), *analysis* (item 5), *standardization* (item 6), and *control* (item 7). Figure 8.5 uses information from many sources as input to determine its output, or contribution to the corporation. Throughout the quality system, SQC and industrial engineering techniques are used to conduct analysis. The output of the analysis is used to develop countermeasures which, once tested, are standardized. Finally, control systems are developed to monitor the process.

Figures 8.8 and 8.9 outline the various activities provided by management services to assist the corporation in attaining *quality assurance* (item 8).

Figures 8.10, 8.11, and 8.12 depict the *effectiveness* (item 9) of management services. Figure 8.10 outlines some of the activities in the effects row (the fifth row). The sixth row of Figure 8.10, effectiveness, outlines the *future plans* (item 10) that were developed at the end of each year as the process was conducted. Management services also has been measuring their output since January 1988 using the systems shown in Figures 8.11 and 8.12.

The actual numbers are confidential and could not be obtained. It is important to note that these systems provide a measurement for a white-collar staff group. At the time this system was developed, very little research had been done in this area. The system forced management services to negotiate valid requirements up front and to query the customer after the project was completed. This improved management services' ability to satisfy its customers.

Figure 8.13, developed in 1989, outlines management services' plan for 1990. Also in 1989, management services was developing detailed plans for 1991 and for five years into the future.

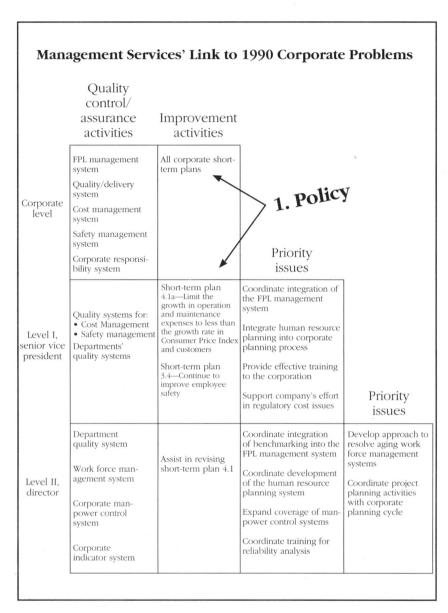

Figure 8.1: Management services policy.

Accountability of the Management Services Department

- Provide control systems to support the corporate objectives of effective utilization of resources and cost control
- Provide staff to support the policy deployment processes and committee, including the investigation and development of recommendations for solution of specific business problems
- Provide consulting support to the corporation in the application of industrial engineering, SQC, and reliability techniques and the development, use, and improvement of quality in daily work control systems
- Provide executive management with timely and appropriately summarized information about company operations

1990 Resources	Management Services	FPL
Operations and maintenance expenses		
Manpower		
Total capital		
During year capital		

CONFIDENTIAL

Juno Beach Office—
Juno Management Services (42)

Miami General Office—
Miami Management Services (25)

Location and customer information

Juno Beach

Miami

Primary Customers

Policy deployment committee
Executive and functional department management

Figure 8.2: Management services statistics.

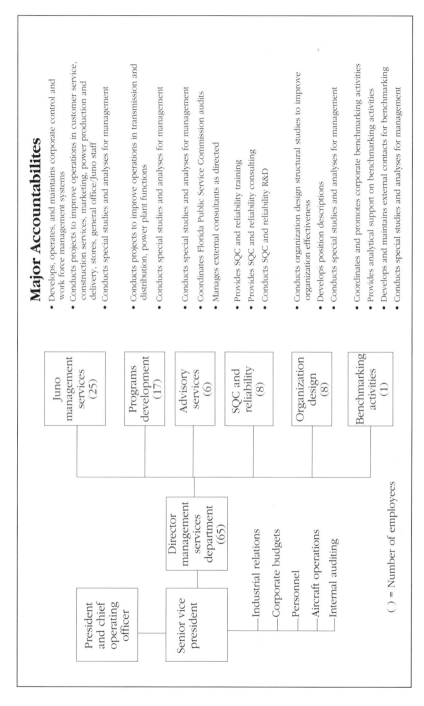

Figure 8.3: Management services organization.

**Organizational Development and Training Classes
Taken or Planned**

Programs development section

Dept. Payroll Loc: 051
Dept. Charge Loc: 029
Date: 8/8/89

Quality Improvement Program Classes

Employee	Techniques I	Application Expert	Leader for Managers I	Leader for Managers II	Leader for Managers III	Supervising Teams	Supervising for Quality	Team Leader
Jose A.	1/88				2/86	3/88	1/88	4/84
Ben	1/89							
Manuel	1/89							4/88
Jose C.	1/89			2/85	2/86		1/88	1/84
Max	1/89							4/88
Dan	1/89						2/87	1/87
Luis		3/89		2/85	2/86	4/88		1/88
Byron	1/89			2/85	2/86			1/88
Jeff	1/89							
Natalie	1/89							
Hank	1/89							3/88
Dinorah								
Penny	1/89							
Steve	1/89							4/82
Bruce	2/85		2/84	1/85		4/88		2/84
Omar	1/89			2/85	2/86			1/88
Fred	1/89		2/85	2/85	2/86	4/88		4/84
Edouard	1/89							

Figure 8.4: Management services education.

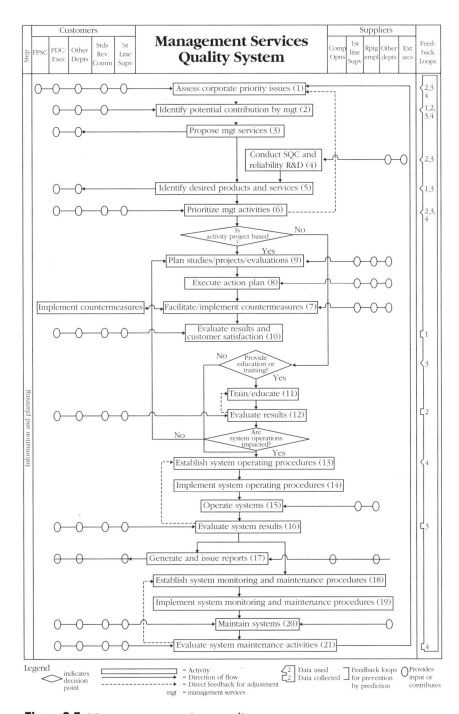

Figure 8.5: Management services quality system.

1. Assess corporate priority issues
   - Identify corporate priority issues
   - Meet with customers
   - Agree on level of need
   - Identify department priority activities
2. Identify potential contribution by management services
   - Match management services to priority issues
3. Propose management services
   - Develop project proposals of selected management services in support of priority issues/problems
4. Conduct SQC and reliability R&D
   - Research new and advanced SQC and reliability techniques
5. Identify desired products and services
   - Agree on valid requirements with customers
   - Establish measurable targets, such as delivery/schedule requirements, resource allocations, etc.
   - Determine reasons for improvement
6. Prioritize management services activities
   - Set priorities based on cross-functional ranking of customer needs and issues such as resource availability and impact on corporate priorities and policy deployment
   - Identify and rank out-of-control systems
7. Plan studies/projects/evaluations
   - Establish approach to address improvement opportunities
   - Establish valid requirements with customer
   - Set project schedule

8. Execute action plan
   - Do the study, create the system, develop procedures, etc., to support the selected countermeasures
9. Facilitate/implement countermeasures
   - Implement recommendations and results of studies/projects
   - Assist the customers in implementing recommendations
10. Evaluate results and customer satisfaction
    - Administer project effectiveness survey and evaluate results
    - Monitor customer indicators
11. Provide training/education
    - Identify educational/skill requirements
    - Develop training classes/programs/materials
    - Provide instructors and/or assist in training instructors
    - Deliver or assist in training
12. Evaluate results of training/education
    - Develop short- and long-term feedback mechanisms
    - Gather customer feedback
    - Evaluate training effectiveness
    - Develop remedial and preventive countermeasures for identified shortcomings
13. Establish system operating procedures
    - Design the procedures, including quality-in-daily-work control systems
    - Establish roles and responsibilities

14. Implement system operating procedures
    - Incorporate procedures into daily work
15. Operate systems
    - Follow established procedures
16. Evaluate system results
    - Monitor system output for accuracy and reasonableness
    - Monitor results of quality-in-daily-work control systems
17. Generate and issue reports
    - Produce reports and distribute to customers
18. Establish system monitoring and maintenance procedures
    - Design computer system procedures and data base maintenance
19. Implement system monitoring and maintenance procedures
    - Incorporate procedures into daily work
20. Maintain systems
    - Modify the data base and computer programs and make minor changes to work standards and allowances
21. Evaluate system maintenance activities
    - Monitor system input versus output
    - Monitor the impact of modifications to work standards

Figure 8.6: Management services quality system activity list.

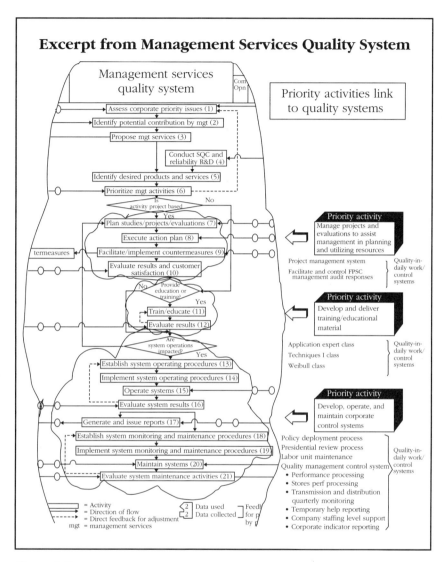

Figure 8.7: Priority activities link to quality system.

Management services is a staff department that provides independent and objective analytical support to management primarily in the areas requiring industrial engineering techniques and SQC and reliability expertise.

The services provided by the department can be summarized into the categories shown below.

Education and training	Evaluations	Project management / Research and development	Products	Systems
Provide SQC training	Conduct tools, material, vehicle, and equipment evaluations	Lead task teams	Develop labor standards	Develop, operate, and maintain corporate control systems
Provide reliability training	Analyze staffing/cost levels and requests	Facilitate task teams	Develop quality-in-daily-work systems	• Corporate manpower control systems
Provide work force management systems training	Analyze management structure	**Research and development**	Provide reliability analyses	• Work force management systems
Provide work method improvement techniques training	Analyze manpower utilization	Conduct SQC R&D	Provide statistical analyses	• Corporate indicator system
Present information on department-related activities	Conduct job analysis/design	Conduct reliability R&D	Develop operations research models	• Corporate policy deployment system
Prepare presentation material on department-related activities	Analyze process flows		Develop planning and scheduling tools	Provide feedback on system results
	Perform training assessments			Provide system data to other systems
	Evaluate application of statistical methods			• Corporate budget systems
	Evaluate application of reliability methods			• Division management information systems
	Conduct verification studies			Facilitate development of corporate management systems
	Analyze facility requirements			• Quality/delivery system
	Analyze management information systems			• Corporate responsibility system
				• Cost management system
				• Safety management system

Figure 8.8: Features and scope of management services.

Legend ◉ = Strong relationship ○ = Moderate relationship △ = Weak relationship	Management Services Link to Corporate Quality Systems Management services priority activity	Develop and deliver training/educational material	Manage projects and evaluations to assist management in planning and utilizing resources	Develop, operate, and maintain corporate control systems
Quality system	Quality system step			
Quality/delivery	Implement mid-term and annual plan through cross-functional management of quality, cost, delivery, safety, and corporate responsibility.	◉	◉	◉
	Control and improvement activities	△	◉	◉
	Develop construction plans for facilities	△	◉	
	Finalize design/joint design review	△	△	
	Construct facilities	△	△	
	Analyze and evaluate design of construction	△	△	
	Establish operating and maintenance standards	△	△	
	Operate facilities	△	△	
	Analyze and evaluate operations	△	△	
	Perform maintenance	△	△	
	Analyze and evaluate maintenance	△	△	
	Establish standards for sales and customer service	△	△	
	Conduct sales activities		△	
	Provide customer service	△	△	
	Handle claims and complaints		△	
	Analyze and evaluate sales and customer service	△	△	
	Understand customer satisfaction and recommend action	△	△	
Employee safety	Analyze and develop/implement countermeasures	△	△	
	Develop and implement countermeasures	△		
	Review effectiveness of countermeasures	△		
Public safety	Assess customer needs and prioritize activities	△		
	Evaluate performance	△		
	Predict future performance and requirements (staff)	△		
	Predict future performance (plant staff)	△		
	Develop detailed projects and action plan	△		
	Review and approve projects	△		
	Review and approve operations standards	△		
	Evaluate operations	△		
	Develop maintenance standards	△		
	Review and approve maintenance standards	△		
	Evaluate maintenance	△		
Corporate responsibility	Assign priorities and lead responsibilities for quality element support and policy review implementation			△
	Plan details of implementation to support policies, corporate short- and mid-term plans, quality element indicator flag systems, and business plans	△	△	△
	Develop action plans/targets/goals in corporate responsibility quality element areas		△	
	Monitor actual performance against plans	△	△	
	Analyze causes, develop and implement countermeasures or improvement actions	△	△	
	Review/approve short-term plans	△		○
	Review results of countermeasures, improvement actions, or short-term plans	△	△	
Cost management	Assess customers' requirements, forecast economic indicators, and assess competition	△	△	
	Identify long-term cost-reduction opportunities		◉	
	Analyze previous short-term plans, financial integrity, and price indicators/targets		◉	
	Draft new short-term plans		◉	○
	Evaluate cost reduction/financial integrity alternatives		◉	
	Identify short-term cost reduction opportunities		◉	
	Translate short-term operational and construction plans into resource requirements		△	○
	Monitor actual performance against plan	△	◉	△
	Analyze deviations, recommend countermeasures, and forecast year-end impact	△	△	

Figure 8.9: Management services link to corporate quality system.

Year / Item	Prior to 1986	1986	1987	1988	1989
Objectives	• Respond to sitcon issues from customers of inflexibility, authority, involvement, and administrative burden	• Identify areas of opportunity for use in backgrounds in QIP • Increase involvement of customers in studies	• Expand involvement in QIP promotion • Increase focus on customer needs	• Integrate QIP into department operations • Continue focus on customer needs	• Align department services to support corporate priorities • Increase customer satisfaction
Develop and deliver training/educational material	• Conducted on-site perf training • Conducted user training classes	• Planned SQC training efforts • Continued user training classes • Trained all staff in LFM III	• Initiated SQC training • Continued user training classes	• Transferred SQC training to QID • Intensified QIP training within management services	• Transferred SQC back to mgt • Increased consulting for SQCR • Targeted SQCR training at specific groups

Manage projects and evaluations to assist mgt in planning and utilizing resources	• Established cross-functional teams on major projects	• Recruited staff with line experience	• Developed project proposal process
			• Began using project initiation letter (contract)
				• Used QI story on projects
				• Used 7 tools and cross-functional teams
				• Developed project management systems
					• Developed process to align dept activities to corp priorities
					• Implemented project mgt system
					  —Project quality
					  —Customer satisfaction

Develop, operate, and maintain corporate control systems	• Eliminated duplicate requisition reviews • Established standards review committee • Developed on-line perf system	• Emphasized resolution of budget issues • Expanded standards review committees (SVC plng/T&D strs) • Increased total office staffing (stores) • Increased staffing flexibility • Developed first QIDW (Perf)	• Expanded standards review committees (G.O. staff) • Piloted average staffing program • Continued to develop QIDW's for major systems	• Focused budget reviews on targets • Promoted average staffing concept • Conducted budget reviews on request • Expanded use of QIDW's • Streamlined requisition process	• Decentralized requisition control • Implemented corp indicator system (new direction for management services) • Piloted self-updating standards
Effects	• Reduced requisition processing time by 50% (14 days to 7 days) • Increased customer acceptance of manpower control systems • Reduced paperwork for customers and improved accuracy	• Increased involvement and understanding of supervisors in manpower control systems • Reduced constraints on line management • Decreased dissatisfaction with budget review process • Developed first QIDW (Perf)	• Reduced dissatisfaction with manpower control systems • Brought systems into control	• Increased use of 7 tools in projects • Reduced requisition processing time further (7 days to 5 days) • Increased customer satisfaction	• Increased managers' understanding of SQC techniques • Targeted corp priority issues • Increased staff support for policy deployment committee • Standardized measures of customer satisfaction
Remaining Problems	• Controls still very centralized • Knowledge of field activities insufficient • Department participation in QIP inadequate	• Customer needs not reflected adequately in project plans • Manpower controls still viewed as restricting management's flexibility	• Use of QI story and 7 tools limited • QIP activities separate from regular work	• Services not fully used on corporate priority systems • Effect of field improvement activities not reflected in control systems in a timely manner • Quality measures on projects not implemented	• Limited use of reliability analyses in problem solving throughout corporation • Project planning activities not coordinated with corporate planning cycle • Workforce management systems aging

Priority activities

Figure 8.10: Management services history of TQM.

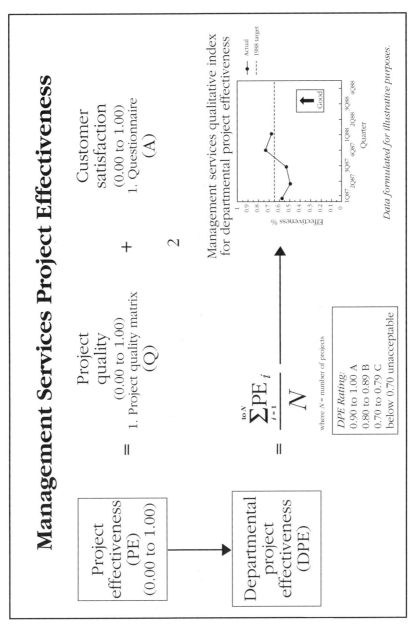

Figure 8.11: Management services qualitative indicator.

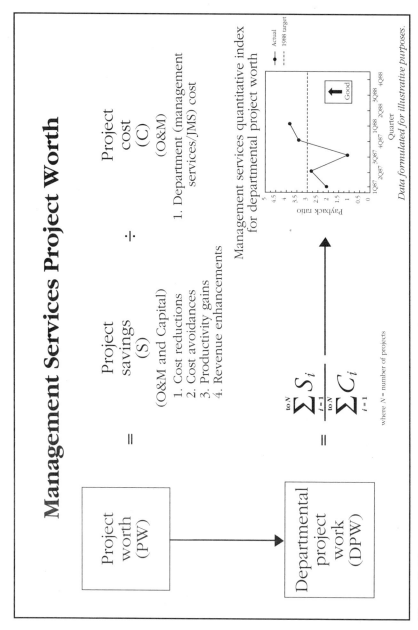

Figure 8.12: Management services quantitative indicator.

Objectives	Level	1990	Assigned to	Completion schedule	Indicator
Develop and deliver training/educational material	I	• Coordinate training for the policy deployment process • Coordinate development of the human resource planning system • Coordinate training for reliability analysis • Design policy deployment training material • Target PD training at specific individuals • Design, develop, and deliver reliability training courses	C D	February January (design/develop) 1st quarter (design/develop) 1st quarter (deliver)	Schedule completion % attendees from target group % target group trained
	II	• Develop approach to resolve aging workforce management systems • Coordinate project planning activities with corporate planning cycle			
Manage projects and evaluations to assist management in planning and using resources	I	• Lead project to develop mid- to long-range human resource planning system	R	2nd quarter	Project effectiveness score
	II	• Integrate department planning activities with corporate planning cycle	A/P	1st quarter	To be determined
Develop, operate, and maintain corporate control systems	I				
	II	• Evaluate alternatives to integrate QIP tools into existing Work Force Management Systems	R	1st quarter	Long-range plan

Priority activities

Figure 8.13: Future plans to address policy issues.

9
Epilogue

The purpose of this text was to develop a procedure that management can use to implement policy deployment for a TQM process. It is evident that the United States is embracing a new management philosophy. The objective of this new philosophy is to achieve customer satisfaction by producing quality goods and services at a reasonable cost. Many organizations are undertaking the task of implementing a TQM process to meet this objective. Implementing policy deployment effectively provides a firm foundation on which to build a TQM process.

A review of existing management systems was followed by an analysis of the current measurement systems for TQM. The Malcolm Baldrige National Quality Award is managed by the U.S. Department of Commerce. It has been in place since 1988 and is awarded annually to U.S. firms meeting specified criteria. Another TQM measurement system is managed by the Union of Japanese Scientists and Engineers (JUSE). JUSE administers the Deming Prize. The Deming Prize has been in existence since 1951.

The Deming Prize criteria used to measure TQM includes the following:

1. Policy
2. Organizational design
3. Education/training
4. Information
5. Analysis
6. Standardization
7. Control
8. Quality assurance

9. Effectiveness
10. Future plans

Each area was researched and a detailed checklist was developed. A comparison of the checklist to a department within FPL was conducted.

A procedure to implement policy deployment for a TQM process was developed. By following this procedure, an organization will develop policy that will guide it in achieving customer satisfaction by producing quality goods and services at a reasonable cost. With many organizations implementing TQM, this procedure will make a significant contribution, if adopted. An example of how effective policy deployment can be is provided through a case study of FPL's policy deployment process. Policy deployment provides an organization with a vision, long-term, mid-term, and short-term management policies, and a system of indicators to track the results. When properly implemented, policy deployment provides every level of the organization with an opportunity to make a quantitative contribution.

Implementing policy deployment in two organizations has taught me a few lessons. In an attempt to keep your journey free of detours, I would like to share these lessons learned.

Executive Commitment

This issue is just about worn out. The fact that senior management must be committed has been well publicized. However, many of my peers are still telling me their senior management is not committed. *If executives of an organization are not committed to TQM, it will not work!*

Adjusting Targets

There are two ways to address a performance gap. One alternative is to allocate resources to identify process improvements and identify root causes to problems. The other alternative is to wave the management magic wand and move the target. Refrain from moving targets. If a legitimate circumstance has arisen, by all means adjust the target. Don't move targets for the sake of looking good. It may seem appropriate behind closed doors, but the customer will know.

Biting Off More Than You Can Chew

The JUSE counselors had a saying: "Even if you could eat an elephant, you still have to eat it one bite at a time." Don't feel like every issue facing your organization has to be a part of your policy deployment. Select issues of a global nature. Choose issues on which everyone in the organization can impact. Less critical issues need to be addressed but do not need to be a part of the overall policy deployment.

Another suggestion is this: in the first year of adopting policy deployment, try to keep the number of short-term management policies between five and seven. It is imperative that the policy deployment process align the organization and move it in the right direction. Selecting too many short-term management policies the first year can spread the organizations resources too thin and cause policy deployment to fail.

Flavor-of-the-Month Syndrome

Rallying around a new process can keep management focused for a period of time. For policy deployment to be effective, the momentum must be maintained. One method to accomplish this is to keep the quality indicators current and well published. Avoid letting your activities fall by the wayside, thus giving the organization a reason to call policy deployment the flavor of the month.

Enjoy the journey!

Notes

Chapter 1

1. Annetta Miller, Frank Washington, Yuriko Hoshari, and Harry Hurt III. "Can the Big Three Get Back in Gear?" *Newsweek* (January 22, 1990): 42.

2. Union of Japanese Scientists and Engineers. *How to Operate QC Circle Activities*. Tokyo: Union of Japanese Scientists and Engineers, 1985, pp. 1–2. Used with permission.

Chapter 2

3. Lester Robert Bittel, Jackson Eugene Ramsey, and Murial Albers Bittel, eds. *Handbook for Professional Managers*. New York: McGraw-Hill, 1985, p. 487. Reprinted with permission of McGraw-Hill, Inc.

4. Michael H. Mescon, Michael Albert, and Franklin Khedouri. *Management, Industrial and Organizational Effectiveness*. New York: Harper and Row, 1981, p. 36.

5. Ibid., 37.

6. Daniel A. Wren. *The Evolution of Management Thought, Second Edition*. New York: John Wiley and Sons, 1979, p. 3. Copyright

©1979 John Wiley and Sons, Inc. Reprinted by permission of John Wiley and Sons, Inc.

7. Ibid., 113. Copyright ©1979 John Wiley and Sons, Inc. Reprinted by permission of John Wiley and Sons, Inc.

8. Mescon, 40.

9. Ibid., 38.

10. Bittel, 491. Reprinted with permission of McGraw-Hill, Inc.

11. Mescon, 41.

12. Mescon, 44.

13. Wren, 323. Copyright ©1979 John Wiley and Sons, Inc. Reprinted by permission of John Wiley and Sons, Inc.

14. Mescon, 35.

15. Wren, 528. Copyright ©1979 John Wiley and Sons, Inc. Reprinted by permission of John Wiley and Sons, Inc.

16. Mescon, 45.

17. Hans G. Daellenbach and John A. George. *Introduction to Operations Research Techniques.* Boston: Allyn and Bacon, 1978, p. 3.

18. Mescon, 47.

19. Mescon, 49.

20. Peter F. Drucker. *The Practice of Management.* New York: Harper and Brothers Publishers, 1954, p. 122.

21. Paul Mali. *MBO Updated, A Handbook of Practices and Techniques for Managing by Objectives.* New York: John Wiley and Sons, 1986, p. 35. Used with permission.

22. Ibid., 92. Used with permission.

23. Mescon, 55.

24. Wren, 462. Copyright ©1979 John Wiley and Sons, Inc. Reprinted by permission of John Wiley and Sons, Inc.

25. Ibid., 509.

26. Mescon, 59.

27. Ibid., 61.

28. John F. Witte. *Democracy, Authority, and Alienation in Work; Workers Participation in an American Corporation.* Chicago: The University of Chicago Press, 1980, p. 41. ©1980 by The University of Chicago. Used with permission.

29. Wren, 359. Copyright ©1979 John Wiley and Sons, Inc. Reprinted by permission of John Wiley and Sons, Inc.

30. Ervin Williams, ed. *Participative Management: Concepts, Theory, and Implementation.* Atlanta: Georgia State University, 1976, pp. 54, 55. Reprinted by permission of Georgia State University Business Press (Atlanta, GA).

31. G. David Garson and Michael Smith, eds. *Organizational Democracy, Participative and Self-Management, Sage Contemporary Social Science Issues 22.* Beverly Hills, CA: Sage Publications, 1976, p. 18. ©1976, reprinted by permission of Sage Publications, Inc.

32. Ibid., 57.

33. Williams, 11.

34. Donald P. Mackintosh, *Management by Exception: A Handbook with Forms.* Englewood Cliffs, NJ: Prentice-Hall, 1978, p. 21. ©1978, reprinted by permission of the publisher, Prentice-Hall, a division of Simon and Schuster, Englewood Cliffs, NJ.

35. Ibid., 35. ©1978, reprinted by permission of the publisher, Prentice-Hall, a division of Simon and Schuster, Englewood Cliffs, NJ.

36. Ibid., 103. ©1978, reprinted by permission of the publisher, Prentice-Hall, a division of Simon and Schuster, Englewood Cliffs, NJ.

37. Alan J. Rowe, Richard O. Mason, and Karl E. Dickel. *Strategic Management and Business Policy: A Methodical Approach.* Reading, MA: Addison-Wesley, 1987, p. 6. ©1987, by Addison-Wesley Publishing Company, Inc. Reprinted with permission of the publisher.

38. Melvin E. Salveson. "The Management of Strategy." *Long Range Planning* (February 1974): 21.

39. David J. Sumanth. *Productivity Engineering and Management; Productivity Measurement, Evaluation, Planning and Improvement in Manufacturing and Service Organizations.* New York: McGraw-Hill, 1984, p. 51. Reprinted with permission of McGraw-Hill, Inc.

40. Johnson Aimie Edosomwan. "A Conceptual Framework for Productivity Planning." *Industrial Engineering* (January 1986): 69.

41. Ibid., 64.

42. William Ouchi. "Going from A to Z: Thirteen Steps to a Theory Z Organization." *Management Review* (May 1981): 9.

Chapter 3

43. Mary Walton. *The Deming Management Method,* with a foreword by W. Edwards Deming. New York: Dodd, Mead and Company, 1986, p. 122.

44. Kaoru Ishikawa. *What Is Total Quality? The Japanese Way,* David J. Lu, trans. Englewood Cliffs, NJ: Prentice-Hall, 1985, p. 37. ©1985 by David J. Lu. Reprinted with permission of the publisher, Prentice-Hall, a division of Simon and Schuster, Englewood Cliffs, NJ.

45. Andrea Gabor. "The Leading Light of Quality, An Innovative Florida Utility Borrows a Page from Japan, Inc." *U.S. News and World Report.* (November 23, 1988): 53.

46. Alan Hodgson. "Deming's Never-Ending Road to Quality." *Personnel Management* (July 1987): 41.

47. Howard S. Gitlow and Shelly J. Gitlow. *The Deming Guide to Quality and Competitive Position,* with a foreword by W. Edwards Deming. Englewood Cliffs, NJ: Prentice-Hall, 1987, p. 20. ©1987, reprinted by permission of Prentice-Hall, Inc., Englewood Cliffs, NJ.

48. Ibid., 29. ©1987, reprinted by permission of Prentice-Hall, Inc., Englewood Cliffs, NJ.

49. Ibid., 102. ©1987, reprinted by permission of Prentice-Hall, Inc., Englewood Cliffs, NJ.

50. Ibid., 130. ©1987, reprinted by permission of Prentice-Hall, Inc., Englewood Cliffs, NJ.

51. Ibid., 144. ©1987, reprinted by permission of Prentice-Hall, Inc., Englewood Cliffs, NJ.

52. Ibid., 157. ©1987, reprinted by permission of Prentice-Hall, Inc., Englewood Cliffs, NJ.

53. Elizabeth Corcoran. "Quality Conscious, Even Techniques for Quality Are Imported." *Scientific American* (July 1989): 75.

54. K. Theodore Krantz. "How Velcro Got Hooked on Quality." *Harvard Business Review* (October 1989): 34.

55. Ibid., 35.

56. Ibid., 40.

57. Norman B. Wright. "Productivity Strategy: Six-Step Approach to Success." *Business Quarterly* (Summer 1985): 10.

58. David A. Garvin. "Quality Problems, Policies and Attitudes in the United States and Japan: An Exploratory Study." *Academy of Management Journal* (December 1986): 660.

59. Ibid., 657.

60. Ibid., 668.

Chapter 5

61. Florida Power and Light Company. *Policy Deployment, How FPL Focuses for Improvement.* Juno Beach, FL: Florida Power and Light Company Quality Improvement Department, 1988, p. 2.

62. Ibid., 5.

63. Ibid., 6.

64. Ibid., 7, 8.

65. Ibid., 9

66. Ibid., 10.

67. Ibid., 10.

Bibliography

Barra, Ralph J. 1983. *Putting Quality Circles to Work*. New York: McGraw-Hill.

Bittel, Lester Robert, Jackson Eugene Ramsey, and Muriel Albers Bittell, eds. 1985. *Handbook for Professional Managers*. New York: McGraw-Hill.

"Building a Quality Improvement Program at Florida Power and Light." 1988. *Target AME's Periodical News Source*. (Fall): 1–10. (Page references are for a reprint.)

Corcoran, Elizabeth. 1989. "Quality Conscious, Even Techniques for Quality Are Imported." *Scientific American* (July): 75–76.

Crosby, P. B. 1984. "In Quest of Quality." *Time* (March 26): 52.

Crosby, Philip B. 1980. *Quality Is Free*. New York: Mentor.

Daellenbach, Hans G., and John A. George. 1978. *Introduction to Operations Research Techniques*. Boston: Allyn and Bacon.

Drucker, Peter F. 1954. *The Practice of Management*. New York: Harper and Brothers Publishers.

Edosomwan, Johnson Aimie. 1986. "A Conceptual Framework for Productivity Planning." *Industrial Engineering* (January): 64–69.

Feigenbaum, Armand V. 1983. *Total Quality Control*. New York: McGraw-Hill.

Fielder, Fred E. 1967. *A Theory of Leadership Effectiveness*. New York: McGraw-Hill.

Florida Power and Light Company. 1988. *Policy Deployment, How FPL Focuses for Improvement*. Juno Beach, Florida: Quality Improvement Department.

Frieman, Jonathan M., and Borje O. Saxberg. 1989. "Impact of Quality Circles on Productivity and Quality: Research Limitations of a Field Experiment." *IEEE Transactions on Engineering Management* (May): 114–118.

Gabor, Andrea. 1988. "The Leading Light of Quality, An Innovative Florida Utility Borrows a Page from Japan, Inc." *U.S. News and World Report* (November 28): 53–56.

Garson, G. David, and Michael Smith, eds. 1976. *Organizational Democracy, Participation and Self-Management. Sage Contemporary Social Science Issues 22*. Beverly Hills, California: Sage Publications.

Garvin, David A. 1986. "Quality Problems, Policies and Attitudes in the United States and Japan: An Exploratory Study." *Academy of Management Journal* (December): 653–673.

Gitlow, Howard S., and Shelly J. Gitlow. 1987. *The Deming Guide to Quality and Competitive Position*. Foreword by W. Edwards Deming. Englewood Cliffs, New Jersey: Prentice-Hall.

Hodgson, Alan. 1987. "Deming's Never-Ending Road to Quality." *Personnel Management* (July): 40–44.

Ishikawa, Kaoru, ed. 1986. *Reports of Statistical Application Research, Union of Japanese Scientists and Engineers, Special Issue: Seven Management Tools for QC*. Tokyo: Union of Japanese Scientists and Engineers, June.

Ishikawa, Kaoru. 1985. *What Is Total Quality Control? The Japanese Way*. Translated by David J. Lu. Englewood Cliffs, New Jersey: Prentice-Hall.

Krantz, K. Theodore. 1989. "How Velcro Got Hooked on Quality." *Harvard Business Review* (October): 34–40.

Lawler, Edward E., III, and Susan A. Mohrman. 1985. "Quality Circles After the Fad." *Harvard Business Review,* (January–February): 65–71.

Mackintosh, Donald P. 1978. *Management by Exception: A Handbook with Forms*. Englewood Cliffs, New Jersey: Prentice-Hall.

Mali, Paul. 1986. *MBO Updated, A Handbook of Practices and Techniques for Managing by Objectives*. New York: John Wiley and Sons.

Mescon, Michael H., Michael Albert, and Franklin Khedouri. 1981. *Management, Individual and Organizational Effectiveness*. New York: Harper and Row.

Miles, Raymond E. 1975. *Theories of Management: Implications for Organizational Behavior and Development,* McGraw-Hill Series in Management. Edited by Keith Davis. New York: McGraw-Hill.

Miller, Annetta, Frank Washington, Yuriko Hoshiai, and Harry Hurt III. 1990. "Can the Big Three Get Back in Gear?" *Newsweek,* (January 22): 42–43.

Mizuno, Shigeru, ed. 1988. *Management for Quality Improvement, The 7 New QC Tools*. Cambridge, Massachusetts: Productivity Press.

Ouchi, William G. 1981. "Going from A to Z: Thirteen Steps to a Theory Z Organization." *Management Review* (May): 8–16.

Ouchi, William G. 1993. *Theory Z: How American Business Can Meet the Japanese Challenge*. New York: Avon.

Peters, Tom. 1987. *Thriving on Chaos*. New York: Alfred A. Knopf.

Rowe, Alan J., Richard O. Mason, and Karl E. Dickel. 1982. *Strategic Management and Business Policy: A Methodological Approach*. Reading, Massachusetts: Addison-Wesley Publishing Company.

Salveson, Melvin E. 1974. "The Management of Strategy." *Long Range Planning* (February): 19–26.

Schonberger, Richard J. 1987. *World Class Manufacturing Casebook, Implementing JIT and TQC*. New York: The Free Press.

Sumanth, David J. 1984. *Productivity Engineering and Management: Productivity Measurement, Evaluation Planning, and Improvement in Manufacturing and Service Organizations*. New York: McGraw-Hill.

Taylor, Frederick W. and Frank B. Gilbreth. 1982. *Principles of Scientific Management: 1911*. Easton, Pennsylvania: Hive.

Union of Japanese Scientist and Engineers. 1986. *The Deming Prize Guide for Overseas Companies*. Tokyo: Union of Japanese Scientists and Engineers.

———. 1985. *How to Operate QC Circle Activities*. Tokyo: Union of Japanese Scientists and Engineers.

———. 1983. *QC Circle Koryo—General Principles of the QC Circle*. Japan: Union of Japanese Scientists and Engineers.

———. No date. *JUSE Organization and Activities*. Tokyo: Union of Japanese Scientists and Engineers.

U.S. Department of Commerce National Bureau of Standards. 1993. *Applications Guidelines 1993 Malcolm Baldrige National Quality Award*. Gaithersburg, Maryland: U.S. Department of Commerce National Bureau of Standards.

Walton, Mary. 1986. *The Deming Management Method*. Foreword by W. Edwards Deming. New York: Dodd, Mead & Company.

Williams, Ervin, ed. 1976. *Participative Management: Concepts, Theory and Implementation*. Atlanta: Georgia State University.

Witte, John F. 1980. *Democracy, Authority, and Alienation in Work: Workers Participation in an American Corporation.* Chicago: The University of Chicago Press.

Wood, Robert Chapman. 1989. "A Lesson Learned and a Lesson Forgotten." *Forbes* (February 6): 70–78.

Wren, Daniel A. 1979. *The Evolution of Management Thought. 2nd ed.* New York: John Wiley and Sons.

Wright, Norman B. 1985. "Productivity Strategy: Six-Step Approach to Success." *Business Quarterly* (Summer): 10–11.

Index